Italian Country Inns & Villas

OTHER BOOKS IN KAREN BROWN'S COUNTRY INN SERIES

FRENCH COUNTRY INNS & CHATEAU HOTELS

ENGLISH, WELSH & SCOTTISH COUNTRY INNS

SWISS COUNTRY INNS & CHALETS

Scheduled for 1987

Spanish Country Inns & Paradors

German Country Inns & Castle Hotels

Austrian Country Inns & Castle Hotels

Italian Country Inns
& Villas

CLARE BROWN

Illustrated by BARBARA TAPP

COLUMBUS BOOKS   London

Copyright © 1985 Travel Press

First published in Great Britain in 1985 by
Columbus Books
Devonshire House, 29 Elmfield Road, Bromley, Kent BR1 1LT

Illustrations, cover design and painting by Barbara Tapp
Maps and calligraphy by Marilyn Krieger

British Library Cataloguing in Publication Data
Brown, Karen
  Italian country inns & villas.
  1. Hotels, taverns, etc.—Italy—Guide-books
  2. Italy—Description and travel—1975—Guide-books
  I. Title
  647'.944501   TX910.I8

ISBN 0–86287–278–2

Printed and bound by R.J. Acford
Chichester, Sussex

TO MY BEST FRIEND, BILL

WITH LOVE and GRATITUDE FOR

MANY MILES OF MEMORIES

Foreword

The style of this book is intended to be more like a comfortable chat with friends than a formal guide – a conversation giving ideas on where to go, what to see along the way, and most important, tips on enchanting little inns to choose for each night to make the trip very special.

And indeed this book is for friends. Our "Inn Series" evolved from planning trips for clients and researching in depth the most charming hotels along the way for them to stay. Through the fun and adventure of researching their holidays, many of these "customers" have become friends, and it is for them, and for you – who share our fondness for "olde worlde" hotels – that we write this guide. We hope through this book the miles will vanish and we can become friends in spirit.

Thank you for your many letters sharing a new favorite hotel, thanking us for a special suggestion, advising us of an inn that is "slipping", or describing a marvelous little restaurant. We delight in your letters and file them all away for future editions.

 # Contents

HOTEL SECTION

INDEX OF HOTELS

Introduction

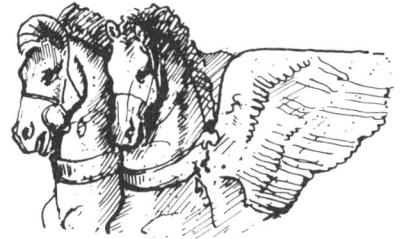

Of all the countries in the world none is more magical for the tourist than Italy. It is truly a tourist's paradise – a traveler's dream destination. No one could be so blase that within Italy's narrow boot there would not be something to tantalize his fancy. For the archaeologist, there are some of the most fascinating and perfectly preserved ancient monuments existing today just begging to be explored. For the gourmet, there is probably the best food in the world. For the outdoorsman, there are towering mountains to conquer and magnificent ski slopes to sample. For the lover of art, the museums are bursting with the genius of Italy's sons such as Michelangelo, Leonardo di Vinci, and Raphael. For the architect, Italy is a school of design – you are surrounded by the ancient buildings whose perfection has inspired the styles of today. For the history buff, Italy is a joy of wonders – her cities are veritable living museums where you are surrounded by the ghosts of Caesar. For the wine connoisseur, Italy produces an unbelieveable selection of wine whose quality is surpassed nowhere in the world. For the adventurer, Italy has intriguing medieval walled villages tucked away in every part of the country just waiting to be explored. For the beach buff, Italy's lakes and islands hold promise of some of the most elegant resorts in the world. For the religious pilgrim, Italy is the cradle of much of the world's faith and home of some of the world's greatest saints. The miracle of Italy is that all these treasures come "packaged" in a gorgeous country of majestic mountains, misty lakes, idyllic islands, wonderful walled villages and gorgeous cities. Plus, the climate is ideal and the people warm and gracious. Italy is truly a delightful destination!

PURPOSE OF THIS GUIDE

This guide is written with two main objectives: to describe the most charming, small, atmospheric hotels throughout Italy and to "tie" these hotels together with itineraries that include enough details so the traveler can plan his own holiday.

Preferences and tastes do vary. This guide does not try to appeal to everyone. It is definitely prejudiced. The hotels included are ones we have seen and liked. It might be a splendid villa elegantly positioned overlooking one of Italy's romantic lakes or a simple little chalet snuggled high in a mountain meadow. But there is a common denominator – they all have charm. Therefore, if you too prefer to travel spending your nights in romantic old villas, charming little chalets, dramatic medieval castles, ancient monasteries, converted peasant's cottages, and gorgeous palaces ... then we are kindred souls and you can follow the paths we have suggested and each night will be an adventure.

HOTEL DESCRIPTIONS

This book is divided into two sections and hotel descriptions are referenced in both. The first portion of the book outlines itineraries and a hotel with a brief description is suggested for each destination. The second section of the book is a complete list of hotels appearing alphabetically by town. In the list is a wide selection of hotels throughout Italy. A brief description, an illustration and pertinent information are provided for each recommendation. These hotels vary tremendously. Some are superb, deluxe, grand hotels fit for a king and very expensive. Other are quite simple little cottages tucked away in remote hamlets and compliment any budget. We include them all if they have "personality," charm, and an antique ambiance. There are a few hotels which are included that do not quite live up to the criteria of "Olde Worlde Charm." The reason they have been included is because in their particular area there just were not "perfect" choices, and since we felt you might need a place to stay — we tried to find the very best possibility.

For some of you, cost will not be a factor if the hotel is outstanding. For others, budget will guide your choices. The appeal of a simple little inn with rustic wooden furniture will beckon some, while the glamour of ornate ballrooms dressed with crystal chandeliers and gilted mirrors will appeal to others. What we have tried to do is to indicate what each hotel has to offer, to describe the setting, so that you can make the choice to suit your own preferences and holiday. We feel if you know what to expect, you will not be disappointed so we have tried to be candid and honest in our appraisals.

HOTEL RATES AND INFORMATION

Hotel rates in Italy are regulated by the government. But, due to inflation and the increased costs of operation, the prices are constantly on the increase. However, the relative values do not change: one budget hotel will still be approximately the same cost as another budget hotel – it's just that they will both be more next year. Conversly, one luxurious hotel will always be in a similar price range with another deluxe hotel. Therefore, since the prices we might quote would be outdated almost before the ink had a chance to dry we have decided to give categories of hotels rather than quote exact lire amounts. We are using the following categories: INEXPENSIVE, MODERATE, EXPENSIVE, VERY EXPENSIVE. In each hotel description we will further indicate special values or pricing situations.

The hotels in the cities, especially in the major tourist areas, are usually relatively more expensive than the same quality of hotel in the countryside or smaller village. Therefore, if you are trying to squeeze the ultimate from your lire, choose hotels in the countryside and take side trips to vist the pricey tourist cites.

Another consideration in Italy is that it is very common in resort areas for the hotels to require a minimum of a three night stay. Sometimes, if the hotel is not full, the manager will accept a last minute booking for one night.

Price is further complicated by the fact that some hotels include meals in the rates and you must dine at the hotel. This of course makes the room rate much higher than for room alone. When a hotel includes breakfast and either lunch or dinner in its rates this is termed half-board. When a hotel rate includes three meals a day this is called full board which might appear expensive, but usually is an excellent value.

Introduction

Some inns seem definitely "adult orientated" and it would appear that children would not be comfortable. Others seem "made for children." Again we have tried to indicate various situations so that you can make an appropriate choice.

CREDIT CARDS

Many small hotels do not accept credit cards. Those hotels which do accept "plastic payment" are indicated in the hotel description section using the following abbreviations: AX = American Express, VS = Visa, MC = Master Charge/Access, DC = Diner's Club, or simply All Major Cards.

ITINERARIES

The first section of this guide outlines itineraries throughout Italy. You should be able to find an itinerary, or section of an itinerary, that can be easily custom tailored to fit your exact time frame and suit your own particular interest. If your time is limited, you could certainly follow just a segment of an itinerary – but, hopefully you will come back for more!

In the itineraries we have not specified numbers of nights at each destination. To do so seemed much too confining. Again, personality dictates what is best for a particular situation. Some travelers like to see as much as possible in a short period of time and do not mind rising with the birds each morning to begin a new adventure. For other travelers, just the thought of packing and unpacking each night makes them shudder in horror and they would never stop for less than three or four nights at any one destination. A third type of tourist doesn't like to travel at all. The destination is the focus and he will use this guide to find the "perfect" resort from which he will never wander except for day time excursions. So once again, use this guide as a reference from which to plan your very own personalized trip.

Please also note that although a hotel is suggested for each destination in an itinerary, that the hotel is just that – a SUGGESTION. Perhaps the hotel seems over your budget, or too fancy, or too simple. Or just not "you." If this is the case just look in the back of the book and choose an alternative.

MAPS

With each itinerary there is a map showing the routing and suggesting places of interest along the way. These are artist's renderings and are not intended to replace a good commercial map. To supplement our generalized routings you will need a set of detailed maps which will indicate all of the road numbers, motorways alternate little roads, motorway access points, exact mileages, etc. Our suggestion would be to purchase a comprehensive selection of both city maps and regional maps before your departure, and with a highlight pen mark your own "personalized" itinerary and pin point you city hotels. (Note: frequently in Italy the hotels do not have a street address – especially in small towns the town itself is the only address. However, in most cases, the tourist bureau does an excellent job of placing signs strategically to guide the tourist to each of the hotels once you are close.) If you live in a metropolitan area you should have no problem buying maps. Personally we find that the Michelin maps are exceptionally good. One reason is that if you want to deviate from an itinerary to explore on your own, Michelin marks in green the most scenic or interesting roads. Michelin maps also tie in with their excellent "Green Guides" which are an outstanding reference for details on when museums are open, etc.

In this book, before the hotel description section, is a map of Italy showing all of the towns in which hotels are recommended. On this map each of the towns is marked with a number indicating its location. These numbers flow geographically across the map to aid you in quickly finding alternate hotels in the area should your first choice be unavailable. These map numbers are cross-referenced in the hotel description section, and the index. Each time a hotel is mentioned the map number is provided.

HOTEL RESERVATIONS

People frequently ask, "Do I need a hotel reservation?" The answer really depends on how flexible you want to be, how tight your time schedule is, which season you are traveling, and how disappointed you would be if your first choice is unavailable.

It is not unusual for the major tourist cities to be completely sold out during the peak season of June through September. Just as this guide was being written, a client wanted assistance with a hotel in Florence. Although we began six weeks in advance it took two days of phone calls contacting at least thirty hotels before we finally found a hotel – in the suburbs! So be forewarned. Hotel space in Rome, Florence and Venice is really at a premium and unless you don't mind taking your chances on a last minute cancellation or staying on the outskirts of a town, make a reservation. Space in the countryside is a little easier. However, if you have your heart set on some special little inn, you certainly should reserve as soon as your travel dates are firm.

Reservations are confining. Most hotels will want a deposit to hold your room and frequently refunds are difficult should you change your plans – especially at the last minute. So it is a double bind. Making reservations locks you into a solid framework, but without reservations you might be stuck with accommodation you do not like!

For those of you who like the security blanket of each night preplanned so once you leave home you do not have to worry about where to rest your head each night, there are several options for making reservations which are listed below.

TRAVEL AGENT: A travel agent can be of great assistance – particularly if your own time is valuable. A knowledgeable agent can handle all of the details of your holiday and "tie" it all together for you in a neat little package including hotel reservations, airline tickets, boat tickets, train reservations, ferry schedules, theatre tickets, etc. For your airline tickets there will be no service fee, but most travel agencies make a charge for their other services. The best advice is to talk with your local agent. Be frank about how much you want to spend and ask exactly what he can do for you and what the charges will be. Although the travel agency in your town might not be familiar with all the little places in this guide, since many are so tiny that they apppear in no other major sources, loan them your book – it is written as a guide for travel agents as well as for individual travelers.

LETTER: If you start early, you can write to the hotels directly for reservations. There are certainly many benefits to this in that you can be specific as to your exact preferences. The important point is to be brief in your request. Clearly state the following: number of people in your party; how many rooms you desire; whether you want a private bathroom; date of arrival and date of departure; ask rate per night; and ask deposit needed. When you receive a reply then send the deposit requested and ask for a receipt. Note: when corresponding with Italy be sure to spell out the month. Mail to Italy is slow. Allow about six weeks for an answer. Although most hotels can understand a letter written in English, on page 191 (just behind the hotel descriptions section) we have provided a reservation request letter written in Italian with an English translation. You can use this as a sample letter or photocopy it and use it for your actual request letters.

TELEPHONE: My preference in making reservations is to call directly. The cost is minimal if you direct dial and you can have your answer immediately. If space is not available, you can then decide on an alternate. Ask you local operator about the best time to call for the lowest rates.

TELEX: If you have access to a telex machine, this is another efficient way to reach a hotel. When a hotel has a telex the number we have included the number in the hotel listing. Again, be sure to be specific as to your arrival and departure dates, number in your party and what type of room you want. And, of course, be certain to include your telex number for their response.

SECURITY WHILE TRAVELING

The Italians make wonderful hosts. They are friendly, outgoing, gregarious and merry. No one is a "stranger". You will experience the feeling that you are a welcome guest in their country.

In spite of the overall graciousness of the Italians, there are a few "misfits" who unfortunately have instilled in many tourists the idea that theft is rampant in Italy. True I have heard stories about purses being snatched and cars pilfered. However, I've heard variations on this same theme with clients returning from Paris, New York, Madrid, and even – I am sorry to admit – from our own town of San Francisco. I have never had the feeling of thieves lurking around every corner ready to spring, and I have never had anything stolen in Italy. Nevertheless, be cautious. In every tourist center – particularly in heavily populated areas such as airports, bus stations, subways, theatres, etc. – the opportunists are about. So watch your purse. Don't let your wallet stand out like a red light in your back pocket. Lock your valuables in the hotel vault. Use travelers checks. Don't leave valuables temptingly exposed in your car. In other words, use common sense – the same as you would at home. By following these simple rules I am sure that you will avoid any unfortunate incidents that could tarnish the perfection of your holiday.

TRAINS

Italy has an excellent network of trains. The major express trains are usually quite reliable and are an extremely efficient way to whip between the major cities. In contrast, the local trains stop at every little town, take much longer, and frequently are completely off schedule.

Each train station is well organized. There is almost always an information desk where someone speaks English who will answer any questions and advise you as to the best schedules. There is another counter where you purchase your tickets. Still a third counter where seat reservations are made.

If you can possibly plan ahead, I strongly recommend purchasing your train tickets in advance. It is quite time consuming to stand in two lines at each train station, only to find – paricularly in summer – that the train you want is already sold out. It is always possible to buy open tickets in the United Kingdom, however, when it is a local train, it is not always possible to purchase, in advance, your seat reservations. When this is the case, go ahead and buy the open tickets and then you can either buy your seat reservations locally, or else pay the concierge at your hotel to handle this transaction for you.

The very popular Eurail Pass is valid in Italy. This is a pass which allows unlimited travel on most trains throughout Europe. However, if you are going to only travel in Italy, then you might want to purchase instead one of the Italian Rail passes which are issued for either 8, 15, 21, 30 days. You can choose either first or second class passes. These passes can be purchased through your travel agent or through the Italian State Railways in London.

Another note on trains – in the summer when rail traffic is very heavy, unless you make dining car reservations in advance you might not be able to have the fun of eating your meal enroute. If you have not made these reservations, as soon as you board the train, zip down to the dining car and ask to reserve a table.

BOATS

Italy has gorgeous islands dotting her shorelines, a glorious string of lakes gracing her mountains to the north, and romantic canals in Venice. Luckily Italy's boat system is excellent – enabling the tourist maximum enjoyment of some of Italy's most stunning destinations.

All of Italy's islands are linked to the mainland and frequently serviced by a wonderful maritime network. The many outlying islands often have overnight ferries which even offer sleeping accommodations and facilities for cars. The closer islands usually have a choice of conveyances – the hydrofoil which zips quickly across the water, or the regular ferry which is slower, but less expensive.

The lakes too have an excellent system of boats. In fact, one of the highlights of traveling in Italy is to explore her glorious lakes, by hopping on one of the ferry boats, which glide romantically between the little villages clustered along the shoreline. Again, there is usally a choice of either the hydrofoil which darts between the hamlets or the ferry which glides leisurely across the water and usually offers beverage and food service on board. The boat schedules are posted at each pier, or you can request a timetable from the Italian tourist office. One note: these little boats are punctual, to the minute, so be right at the pier with your ticket in hand so you can jump on board during the brief interlude that the boat huddles at the shore.

If at all possible squeeze in a short boat excursion while in Italy. It is a treat you will remember and it will enhance your trip.

WEATHER

Italy is blessed with lovely weather. However, unless you are a ski enthusiast following the promise of what the majestic mountains have to offer in the winter, or must travel in summer due to school holidays, I highly recommend traveling in spring or fall. Travel at either of these times has two dramatic advantages: you miss the rush of the summer tourist season when all of Italy is packed, and you are most likely to have beautiful weather. In spring the meadows are painted with wildflowers and in fall the forests are a riot of color as the trees ready for winter.

WHAT TO WEAR

During the day informal wear is most appropriate including comfortable slacks for women. In the evening, if you are at a sidewalk cafe or a simple pizzaria, women do not need to dress up nor men to wear coats and ties. However, Italy does have some elegant restaurants, and definitely a dress and coat and tie are the proper wear. I think a basic principle is to dress as you would in any city at home. There are perhaps a few special situations. The churches are still very conservative and shorts are definitely inappropriate. In fact, some of the cathedrals still insist that women have their arms covered. It is rare that a scarf on the head is required, but to wear one is a respectful gesture.

The "layered" effect is ideal for Italy. Because Italy's climate runs the gamut from always cool in the mountains to frequently very hot in the south, the most efficient wardrobe is one where light blouses and shirts can be "reinforced" by layers of sweaters which can be added or peeled off as the day demands.

SHOPPING

Italy is a shopper's paradise. Not only are the stores brimming with tempting merchandise, but their displays are beautiful from the tiniest fruit market to the most chic boutique. Some of the favorite items to buy include the following: shoes, handbags, gloves, suitcases, leather goods of all kinds, gold jewelry, coral, religious items, silk ties & scarves, lithographs, perfume, blow glass, handmade lace, and designer dresses & suits.

Introduction

FOOD and DRINK

It is almost impossible to get a bad meal in Italy. Italians themselves love to eat and seem to make dining a social occasion to be with family and friends. So the restaurants are filled not only with tourists but with the Italians who dawdle at the tables long after the meal is over chatting and laughing with perhaps a glass of wine or a last cup of coffee.

You will soon get in the spirit of the game of deciding which kind of restaurant to choose for your next meal – and the selection is immense, all the way from the simple family trattoria where mama is cooking in the kitchen to the most elegant of gourmet restaurants with world renowned chefs. Whichever you choose, you will not be disappointed.

Thank you, Marco Polo, for importing from China the art of making pasta. It now is the mainstay of any meal prepared in a fascinating, endless array of culinary delights.

Wine of course is served with every meal. You rarely see an Italian family eating without their bottle of wine on the table. Unless you are a true wine connoisseur I suggest the regional wines. If you ask your waiter to assist you with the choice, you will flatter him and discover many superb wines. Some of the most popular wines which you will see on the Italian menus are CHIANTI, a popular wine produced in the Tuscany area south of Florence; MARSALA, a golden sweet wine from Sicily; SOÁVE, a superb light wine produced near Venice; ORVIETO, a semi-sweet wine from the Umbria area near Assisi, and EST EST EST, a beautiful semi-sweet wine produced near Rome. The story that I hear about the last wine, Est Est Est, is lots of fun and perhaps even true. It seems that a wealthy man was traveling south and being a true gourmet both of food and drink, he sent his servant before him to pick out all the best places to eat along the way. When the servant neared Rome he found such a divine wine that all he could relay back to his master was EST EST EST, which as you students of Latin will remember means Yes Yes Yes! And the wine is definitely still "Yes Yes Yes" as are most that you will have the joy of drinking in Italy!

DRIVING

PETROL: Petrol is very expensive so plan ahead and budget this as part of your trip if you are driving. If you purchase a car in Europe and it is registered in a country other than Italy, you can purchase petrol discount coupons at the border.

ROADS: The Italian roads are nothing short of spectacular, and are some of the finest in the world. In fact, the Italians are absolute geniuses when it comes to their engineering feats (which actually is not surprising when you think what a fantastic road system the Romans built two thousand years ago!). Nothing seems to daunt them where roads are concerned. You would think the mountains were of clay instead of solid rock the way they tunnel through them for miles on end. Nothing seems too expensive or too much trouble where roads are concerned. Sometimes a roadway will be seemingly suspended forever in mid air, as it spans an ocean gorge or bridges a mountain crevasse.

TOLL ROADS: Italy has a network of super motorways that draws the whole country into an easily manageable destination by car. Once you are on the toll roads the miles whip by and you can go quickly from almost any area of Italy to another most efficiently. However be forewarned. These toll roads are very expensive. It seems that about every half hour a toll station appears and you owe another couple of pounds. But it is worth it. Every penny is well spent when you consider the alternative of creeping along within a maze of trucks and buzzing motorcycles taking forever to go only a few miles. Take the toll roads for the major distances you need to cover, and then choose the small roads when you wish to leisurely meander through the countryside.

The Toll Roads are a little confusing until you learn the system – even then it is confusing because just when you think you have the operation "down pat" you will find it varies slightly. But this is the most common routine. First follow the green motorway signs toward the toll road. Sometimes these signs begin miles from the road so be patient and continue the game of "follow the sign." Each entrance to the motorway handles traffic going in both directions. As you enter into the toll gate there is usually a red button you push and a card pops out of a slot. After going through the toll station you choose the direction you want to go. Leaving the motorway there will be a toll station where your ticket will be collected and you will pay according to how many miles traveled.

ROAD SIGNS: Before starting on the road prepare yourself by learning the international driving signs so that you can obey all the rules of the road and avoid the embarrassment of heading the wrong way down a small street or parking in a forbidden area! There are several basic sign shapes. The triangular signs warn that there is danger ahead. The circular signs indicate compulsory rules and information. The square signs give information concerning telephones, parking, camping, etc. To acquaint you, some of the more common signs are listed below.

No entry for pedestrians	No animals	No entry for all motor vehicles	End of no overtaking	No overtaking for lorries	End of no overtaking

Danger! Level crossing	Low-flying aircraft	Falling rocks	Cross-wind	Quayside or river bank	Two-way traffic

Give way	Slippery road	Uneven road	Steep hill - descent	Tunnel	Opening bridge

Right bend	Left bend	Double bend	Dangerous bend	Cross roads	Roundabout traffic

Introduction

| End of all restrictions | Halt sign | Halt sign | Customs | No stopping | No parking/waiting |

| Mechanical help | Filling station | Telephone | Camping site | Caravan site | Youth hostel |

| All vehicles prohibited | No entry for all vehicles | No right turn | No U-turns | No entry for motorcars | No overtaking |

| Road works | Loose chippings | Level crossing with barrier | Level crossing without barrier | Maximum speed limit | End of speed limit |

| Traffic signals ahead | Pedestrians | Children | Animals | Wild animals | Other dangers |

| Intersection with non-priority road | Merging traffic from left | Merging traffic from right | Road narrows | Road narrows at left | Road narrows at right |

Introduction

19

Italian
Highlights
by Train & Boat

MILAN
SIRMIONE
Lake Garda
Riva
Desenzano
VERONA
Padua
VENICE
FLORENCE
ROME
Naples
Pompei
CAPRI
SORRENTO

ITALIAN HIGHLIGHTS BY BOAT AND TRAIN

This itinerary can be journeyed easily by car; however, just the thought of taking an automobile onto an Italian expressway intimidates some of the bravest breed of tourist.   I must admit that the Italians love cars and enjoy driving fast; it would seem that many are practicing for the Grand Prix.   But an aversion to driving does not mean that your only alternate is a "package" tour.   Italy can be seen splendidly by train and boat.   This is a glorious way to travel and has many advantages such as: no one needs to watch the road instead of the scenery; family crises that occur when the map reader fails to notice the vital turn off sign until it has zipped past can be avoided; a bottle of wine can be savoured with lunch; and everyone arrives rested and ready to enjoy the sights!   But maybe the best advantage of all is that while using local transportation you will make friends.   Perhaps there will be just a smile at first, then maybe the sharing of a piece of fruit, or later, the admiration of each other's family photographs. Somehow barriers break down on a long journey and the universal warmth of friendliness - at which the Italians are masters - spans the language barriers.

Italian Highlights

This itinerary covers some of the most famous destinations within Italy. For a short holiday it is impossible to include all the places of interest, but following this pathway will easily provide you with a glimpse of some of the highlights of Italy and will hopefully tempt you to quickly return to delve more deeply into the wonders that Italy has to offer. This itinerary is woven around towns that are conveniently linked by public transportation. Of course, if your time is extremely limited, this itinerary lends itself well to segmentation. If you cannot travel with us all the way, then choose what fits into your schedule and what most appeals to you personally. No matter what portion you include, you will be treated to a delightful holiday.

In the following itinerary approximate train and boat times have been included. Please note that these are given only as a reference to show you how the pieces of this itinerary tie together. Schedules are constantly changing, so these must be verified. Also, many boats and some trains are seasonal, so be very meticulous in making your plans.

ORIGINATING CITY   MILAN

This highlight tour begins in Milan, a most convenient city since it is the hub of airline flights from throughout Europe, plus is blessed with non-stop air service from the United States. Also, Milan is strategically located for trains arriving from all over Europe. Into her busy station, trains come rushing via the Gotthard, Simplon and Bernina passes. However, it is not her location alone which makes Milan an ideal starting point. Although frequently bypassed as an enormous industrial city, Milan has at her core a truly charming metropolis which incorporates delights to please all tastes: some of the best shopping in Italy gorgeously displayed in glass-domed arcades, superb medieval squares snuggled unexpectedly within her boundaries, dazzling cathedrals, superb museums, gourmet restaurants, and of course, La Scala - probably the most famous opera house in the world.

DESTINATION I   SIRMIONE   Villa Cortine Palace Hotel

═══

1:00 PM Depart Milan by train
2:20 PM Arrive Desenzano

NOTE: This train usually departs from the Milan Central Station, but sometimes the trains depart instead from the Porto Garibaldi station, so it is vital that schedules be checked very carefully.

When the train arrives in the ancient port of Desenzano, you can take a cab to the pier where the hydrofoils, steamers and buses leave for Sirmione. However, although more expensive, taking a cab directly to Sirmione (only about six miles away) is a splurge but also it is really the most convenient means of transportation since you can be taken directly to your hotel.

SIRMIONE is a walled medieval village fabulously located on a tiny peninsula jutting out into Lake Garda - actually almost an island because you first drive along a narrow thread of land and then magically enter Sirmione across the moat through the medieval gates! Unless you are one of the lucky ones with a hotel for the night, you will not be allowed to enter by car since pedestrians only are allowed through the entrance. But with hotel reservations, you can stop at the information office near the entrance and be given a pass to enter by car.

There are several hotels in the heart of Sirmione but the most glamorous choice, the VILLA CORTINE PALACE HOTEL, is located in a gorgeous park on the outskirts of town. The entrance is absolutely "Hollywood." You must ring a bell at the impressive gates which then slowly swing open allowing you to wind your way up through the truly beautiful park to the hotel which crowns the small hill. Previously, this was a sumptuous private villa. Now a new wing has been built which doubles the original size. Although the newer wing looks from the outside a bit sterile, the rooms are delightful and most have better views than those in the old section. Demi-pension (breakfast and dinner) are required if you are staying at the Villa Cortine Palace. In addition, reservations are usually only taken for stays of at least three nights. But neither should prove a problem - you will never want to leave such a delightful setting!

Villa Cortine Palace
Sirmione

From the Villa Cortine Palace Hotel you can easily walk to the wharf in the middle of town and study the boat schedule in order to make the delightful decision of which boat you want to take for your day's excursion. You can either glide around the lake all day and have a snack on board, or you can get off in some small jewel of a town and enjoy lunch at a lakefront cafe.

There is also a small train, similar to those we have in some of our parks, which shuttles back and forth to the tip of the peninsula, so that those who prefer riding to walking can visit the small church and the Roman Ruins.

DESTINATION II   VERONA   Hotel due Torri

===

There are trains almost every hour that cover the half hour journey between Desenzano and Verona.   But if it is a beautiful day it might be much more fun to incorporate some sightseeing into your transportation and take a boat and bus instead. If so, the following gives an idea of how this can be done.

9:50 AM Depart Sirmione by ferry
1:25 PM Arrive Riva

You can have lunch on board the ferry or else you can wait until you reach the medieval town of RIVA, located on the northern shore of Lake Garda.   The terrace overlooking the lake at the Hotel Sole, located just across from where the ferry docks, provides a serene luncheon setting.   The ancient section of Riva is very small, so it will not take long to stroll the small square before you take one of the buses.   These leave fifteen times a day in summer for the ride along the eastern shore of the lake and then go on to Verona.

When you arrive in VERONA you will be delighted.   This is a town all too frequently bypassed, but what a prize!   The city is oozing with medieval charm and proudly boasts one of the most marvelous Roman amphitheaters in Italy - and that is saying a lot!   Luckily, Verona has several excellent hotels to complement her marvelous sights.   A delightful choice would be the ALBERGO DUE

TORRI. It is is strategically situated for walking, and offers much more than just location. One of the fun and unique attributes of the hotel is the decor of its bedrooms. They all vary and if the hotel is not full there is a clever slide presentation in the lobby where you can choose the bedroom decor to suit your mood. Each of the bedrooms is furnished in genuine antiques, usually quite ornate and elegant from the 19th century.

Hotel due Torri
Verona

DESTINATION III   VENICE   Gritti Palace

When you are ready to leave Verona, there is frequent train service to Venice so the following is just a suggestion.

1:15 PM depart Verona by train
2:56 PM arrive Venice, Santa Lucia station

As you come out of the front door of the train station you will find that the station is directly on the Grand Canal and that it is a few short steps down to where one boards a boat to take you to your hotel. The VAPORETTO is the most popular means of transportation and is very inexpensive. This is like a "boat bus" which constantly shuttles back and forth from the train station to St. Mark's Square. The Number Two bus only makes major stops and the Number One bus hesitates at every stop to exchange passengers. Much more expensive, but a little faster, is the MOTOSCAFI which is like a taxi and will take you wherever you want to go provided there is a motor boat dock. The GONDOLAS are much slower and even more expensive. (I would save my gondola ride for a more romantic interlude than a train connection!)

VENICE has many wonderful hotels in every price range. For this itinerary, perhaps the best is the GRITTI PALACE, a former home of the immensely wealthy Doge Andrea Gritti! And, indeed, you can believe it as you arrive in style at the hotel's dock on the Grand Canal and descend in grandeur onto the red carpet, past the diners enjoying a snack on the deck, and into the beautiful lobby. If price is of no matter, go all the way and request a room overlooking the canal.

Hotel Gritti Palace
Venice

Italian Highlights

Venice has so many sights: marvelous restaurants, beautiful boutiques, and fascinating little alley ways to explore that you could happily stay for weeks. Of course, you will want to savour all the ambiance of St. Mark's Square and visit the Doges' Palace. See the Clock Tower whose huge bronze figures bang out the hours with massive hammers. Wander through the museums. Go either on your own or on a tour to the three islands of MURANO (famous for its hand blown glass), BURANO (famous for its colorfully painted fishermen's cottages and the making of lace), and TORCELLO (once an important city but now just a small village with only its lovely large church to remind one of its past glories.) A real bargain is to board the Vaporetto and enjoy the many wonderful palaces bordering the Grand Canal. My favorite recommendation in Venice is wandering - just anywhere - exploring the maze of twisting canals and criss-crossing back and forth over some of the four hundred toy-like bridges.

Another outing you will certainly enjoy is to take the IL BURCHIELLO, named for a famous Seventeenth Century Venetian boat, which leaves Tuesdays, Thursdays, and Saturdays at about 9:20AM from Pontile Giarinetti pier at St. Mark's square and travels the network of rivers and canals linking Venice and Padua. (The schedule might change, so verify.) This little boat, with an English speaking guide on board, stops at several of the exquisite palaces enroute. Lunch is served and there is time for sightseeing in Padua before returning to Venice by bus. This is a delightful excursion.

DESTINATION IV   FLORENCE   Lungarno Hotel

There are several direct trains each day from Venice to Florence; however, in summer, space is at a real premium, so be sure to reserve a seat in advance. Some of the express trains must have prior seat reservations and will require a supplemental fee.   NOTE: if you want to dine on the train, it is necessary, during the busy season, to make reservations in advance when you buy your ticket.

11:00 AM depart Venice, Santa Lucia station, (train "Marco Polo")
2:14 PM arrive Florence

In FLORENCE, stay perhaps at the LUNGARNO HOTEL, which rises directly from the banks of the Arno very near the Ponte Vechio.   The Lungarno is not an "Olde Worlde" hotel, but rather a modern, very tastefully decorated, charming hotel perched directly on the Arno only steps from the heart of Florence. Although new, the Lungarno happily qualifies without too much stretch of imagination for our inn series because it incorporates into its construction a 13th century tower in which there are some romantic rooms.   However, my preference would be a room in the front overlooking the river - a few even have balconies for those lucky travelers who book well in advance!

Be generous with your time and do not rush Florence.   There is too much to see. You must, of course, pay a visit to Michelangelo's DAVID in the Accademia (located just off the Piazza San Marco), and you must not miss the fantastic museums and cathedrals - the world will probably never again see a city which has produced so much artistic genius!   Travelers best appreciate Florence when they are simply roaming.   Wander through the streets and poke into small boutiques.   Stop in churches which catch your eye - they all abound with masterpieces.   Sit to enjoy a cappuchino in one of the little sidewalk cafes and "people watch."   Stroll through the piazzas and watch some of the artists at work - many of them incredibly clever - as they paint portraits and do sculptures for a small fee.   End your day by finding the perfect small restaurant for a delicious pasta made by mama in the back kitchen.

Lungarno Hotel
Florence

DESTINATION V   ROME   Forum Hotel

There is excellent train service from Florence to Rome.   It is probably best to take one of the mid-day trains which will allow you to enjoy lunch as you soak in the beauty of the Tuscany hills flowing by your window.   Remember that you will need both seat and dining reservations.

11:23   AM depart Florence via train "the Stebello"
 2:04   PM arrive Rome Termini Station

As the train pulls into the enormous city of ROME, you will feel overwhelmed by its size, but once you settle into the FORUM and go up to the delightful rooftop terrace for a panoramic view of the city, you will be highly motivated to begin the exploration of this fabulous city of archaeological wonders.

Rome is bursting with a wealth of fantastic museums, ancient monuments, spectacular cathedrals, gourmet restaurants, beautiful boutiques, colorful piazzas, whimsical fountains, inspiring statues, theatre, opera...the city itself is a virtually a museum! One cannot possibly savour it all. Do get an excellent guidebook and decide what is top priority for your own special interests. If there are several in your party, then a private guide might be money well spent since he will custom tailor your sightseeing.

Forum Hotel
Rome

DESTINATION VI   SORRENTO   Grand Excelsior Vittoria

One could spend weeks discovering the museum that is Rome, but if you have time to add a few more highlights before your return, try to include Sorrento and Capri.

There is frequent train service from Rome to Naples and from there it is a short

ALISCAFI (hydrofoil) ride to Capri.   However, for the adventurous it is fun to
include Pompei and Sorrento enroute.   Please be advised that this makes a long
day of travel and takes some manipulating of schedules but the rewards are
great!

You will need an early start to accomplish a tour of Pompei on your way to
Sorrento, but this is a must.   How could you be so close to this intriguing city of
the Romans which was frozen in time by the ashes of Vesuvius without a visit?

 8:50 AM depart Rome Termini Station
11:46 PM arrive Pompei Main Station

You ARRIVE in Pompei at the main station, but you will DEPART from Pompei
at the Villa d. Misteri Station, located just across from the main entrance to the
archaeological site.   Since you will need to store your baggage while you
sightsee, I suggest taking a cab from the Main Station to the Villa d. Misteri
station and checking your suitcases.   Then you can just walk across the street to
the main gate of Pompei.   There is a nice terrace restaurant by the entrance
and also a cafe inside.   If you want to do your own touring, you can buy an excellent guide-book in English from a stall, or else you can negotiate with one of the
licensed guides for a personal tour.

You may have heard that the earthquake of 1980 destroyed much of Pompei.   It
is true that many of the sites were damaged and some are still under reconstruction, but do not worry, there is still enough to keep you busy for hours.   An aura
of mystery lingers in the air as you wander the streets of Pompei.   All are
touched by this ancient city which, in one day, was frozen for all time.

As you explore Pompei, there is no need to watch your clock because there is a
fun, narrow gauge train departing from the Pompei Villa dei Misteri station
about every twenty minutes for the half-hour scenic journey to Sorrento.

When you arrive in SORRENTO, stay at the GRAND HOTEL EXCELSIOR VITTORIA, a romantic old villa at the center of town in a prime cliff location overlooking the harbor. The hotel's once perfect grandeur is perhaps a bit faded, but as you sit on the terrace in the evening and watch the sun turning the bay into shades of red and gold, the atmosphere is perfection. There is also a pool for relaxing and sunning. Definitely ask for a deluxe room with a view so that you can squeeze the ultimate experience from this fantastic setting.

Grand Hotel Excelsior Vittoria
Sorrento

DESTINATION VII   CAPRI   Grand Hotel Quisiana

When it is time to leave Sorrento there is excellent service by either hydrofoil or ferry to Capri. Perhaps the following schedule will give you a suggestion:

5:45 PM depart Sorrento by hydrofoil
6:30 PM arrive Capri

Your hydrofoil will arrive at the Marina Grande where you will find major hotel representatives on the pier. They will relieve you of your luggage and take it directly to your room. You can then walk over to take either a mini-bus or the funicular to the main town of CAPRI.

There are many small hotels on Capri but, if you want to splurge, a deluxe hotel choice is the GRAND HOTEL QUISIANA. A larger hotel than most recommended in this guide, it is an oasis at the heart of Capri where you can retreat to a haven during the heat of the day and relax by the beautiful pool. During the day, the island is swarming with tourists who come on day tours. I used to think that in the evening the activity subsided. This isn't so! The tour groups leave at dusk but from the deluxe villas and fancy hotels a new group emerges in their chic clothes and fancy jewelry to stroll the streets - there both to see and be seen.

Capri has many wonders. The most famous is its submerged cave, the BLUE GROTTO, which can be reached by boat when the seas are calm. Large boats begin leaving the harbor every morning at 9:00 AM for the short ride to the entrance to the Blue Grotto. There you will be transferred into tiny row boats. The excursion is an adventure in itself. As your little boat approaches the tiny cave opening it seems impossible there will be adequate room, but suddenly the sea surges forward and in you squeeze. Like magic you see it - the mysterious stunning blue light reflecting from some hidden source which illuminates the grotto.

Capri is also a marvelous island for walking. As you stroll the trails, all your senses will be treated by the fragrant flowers, the gorgeous vistas of the brilliant blue waters and the sound of birds luring you ever onward. There are many spectacular walks. Follow the trail winding down the cliffs to the small harbor on the opposite side called MARINA PICCOLA. There are lovely views of the shimmering aqua waters as you make your way to the small beach where you can enjoy a swim before your return.   Instead of walking back up the hill, take the little bus which will deliver you quickly back to the main square.

Another absolutely spectacular walk - although a long one of at least forty-five minutes each way - is to Emperor Tiberius' palace, perched high on the cliffs on the western tip of the island.   From there the view is incredible!   You can have an overview of the whole island plus watch the ferries shuttling back and forth to the mainland.   This spot among the ruins makes the perfect picnic place, so pack a feast of famous Italian salami, cold pasta salad and crisp, fruity soave wines, and soak in the view!

A much shorter walk, but one equally as beautiful, is to the Cannone Belvedere. This tiny walkway guides you near delightful private villas hidden behind high walls (you can get glimpses through the gates) and on to a promontory overlooking the sea.

When the real world calls and you must leave Capri, there is frequent ferry or hydrofoil service back to Naples.   From there, you can either take a train to Rome or a plane to your next destination.

Grand Hotel Quisiana
Capri

Italian Highlights

Mountain and Lake Adventures

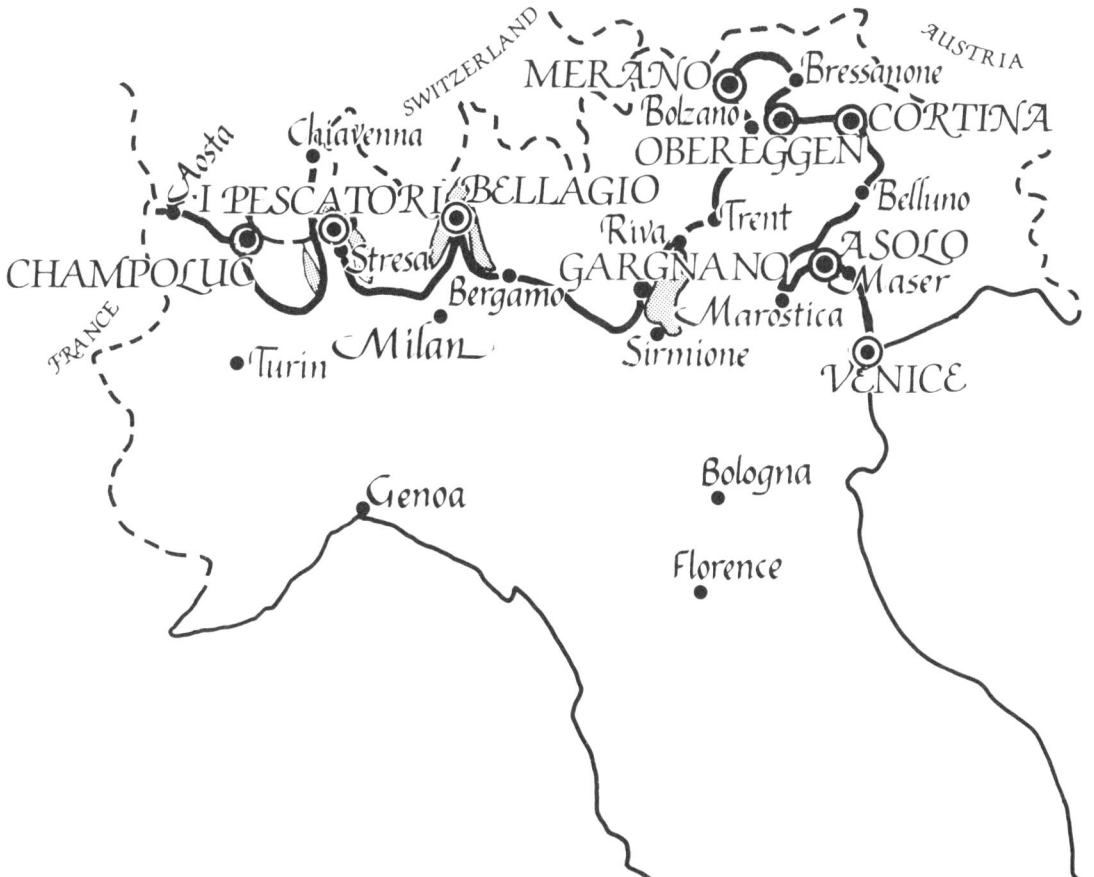

AUSTRIA

SWITZERLAND

FRANCE

Aosta

Chiavenna

MERANO

Bressanone

Bolzano

CORTINA

OBEREGGEN

I PESCATORI

BELLAGIO

Belluno

CHAMPOLUC

Stresa

Riva

Trent

ASOLO

Bergamo

GARGNANO

Maser

Turin

Milan

Sirmione

Marostica

VENICE

Genoa

Bologna

Florence

MOUNTAIN & LAKE ADVENTURES

For the traveler who wants to combine the magic of seeing some of the world's most splendid mountains with the joy of visiting Italy's gorgeous northern lakes, this itinerary will be ideal.   Contrasts will heighten the impact of visual delights as you meander across Northern Italy through lovely mountain passes, through lush green meadows laced with wildflowers, beneath giant mountains piercing the sky with their jagged granite peaks, and bordering lazy blue lakes whose steep shorelines are decorated with endearing little Italian villages wrapped in misty cloaks of wonderful sienas and ochres.   What a glorious holiday to wind across Northern Italy enjoying some of her most beautiful landscapes.   This itinerary can delightfully stand alone.   However, it is also perfect for the traveler arriving or departing from neighboring countries.   We have carefully shown deviations for the tourist who will be leaving or entering from Austria, Switzerland, or France.   All too often the tourist thinks he has "finished" Italy when his tour ends in Venice and he too quickly rushes north into Austria or Switzerland.   What a waste!   A very promising picturesque region still remains.   Please try to linger to enjoy some of the mountains and lakes which truly are some of Italy's greatest natural artistic treasures.

Mountain & Lake Adventures

ORIGINATING CITY   VENICE

This itinerary begins in Venice, one of the most romantic cities in the world. Her maze of waterways are criss-crossed by storybook little bridges and shadowed by majestic palaces whose soft hues warmly reflect in the shimmering water. Here black gondolas quietly glide through the minute canals as the gondolier in his red and white stripped shirt softly seranades his romantic passengers with an operatic selection. Venice is not a traditional city, rather an archipelago of one hundred seventeen islands "glued" together by four hundred bridges.

DESTINATION I   ASOLO   Villa Cipriani

You need not rush your departure this morning. Venice is a city that should be slowly enjoyed and since your journey today is short, you can certainly have the luxury of a last leisurely breakfast before embarking on your next adventure.

Since all the "streets" in Venice are liquid, you will need to take a boat to your car. It will probably be at the PIAZZALE ROMA where most of the car rental companies are located, in addition it is also where there are overnight car parks for storing your car if you drive into Venice. The choice of conveyance will depend upon your budget and your inclination. The VAPORETTO is the most reasonable. Similar to a river bus the Vaporetto leaves regularly from St. Mark's Square for the approximately half hour ride to the Piazzale Roma. The Vaporetto Number One stops at most of the little docks along the route whereas Vaporetto Number Two is an express boat which stops at only a few major points.

The MOTOSCAFO are motorboats which duck through the back canals and usually take about fifteen minutes to Piazzale Roma. The Motoscafo are like private cabs and are much more expensive than the "bus," but can be very convenient, especially if your hotel has a private motor boat landing. The most deluxe mode of transportation is by private GONDOLA; however, these are very expensive and usually take about an hour to reach Piazzale Roma.

Once you have retrieved your car from the parking garage or have finished the paper work for your car rental, head north from Venice toward TREVISO which requires about an hour's drive. If time allows, try to stop in Treviso. Stroll through this picturesque city spider-webbed with canals and surrounded by 15th century ramparts. Perhaps have a cup of coffee or a bite of lunch before heading north toward Asolo. Treviso is famous for its arcaded streets, churches lavishly decorated with frescoes, and many delightfully painted houses. You might want to climb the ramparts for a view of the Alps beckoning you on.

Villa Cipriani
Asolo

From Treviso it is approximately another hour to Asolo. However, just a few miles before you reach Asolo you should see signs for the town of MASER where the marvelous VILLA DI MASER (some of your books might use the name of VILLA BARARO) is located. This is a splendid villa designed by Palladio and fabulously decorated with frescoes by Paolo Veronese. This elegant villa has erratic days and hours when it is open to the public - usually in late afternoons on Tuesdays, Saturdays and Sundays. However, it is only about one mile out of your way, so well worth a detour to investigate. There is also a very interesting museum of old carriages and antique cars at Villa di Maser.

Your prize tonight is ASOLO. Asolo is an absolute delight. It is a gem of a small medieval village snuggled on the side of a hill with lovely views of the countryside. As you drive toward Asolo the terrain does not seem to hold much promise - just modern towns and industry - but then the signs point to Asolo and the road winds up a lovely hillside and into the tiny village which encompasses a delightful combination of a "real" town with its gorgeous fruit stands, candy shops, colorful little grocery store, etc. for those lucky few who live in Asolo; plus, gorgeous shops with beautiful merchandise for the tourist. Of course a castle adorns the hill above the village - mostly in ruins but setting the proper stage. Naturally, there is a wonderful cathedral dominating the square, just as it should. You will find all this plus vineyards and olive trees on the hillsides and the scent of roses in the air. No wonder Robert Browning fell in love with Asolo and chose it as his home. It might not be possible for all to live in Asolo, but you will have the marvelous option of the VILLA CIPRIANI which is a superb villa (once the home of Robert Browning) where you too can pretend that Asolo is yours. Sit on the lovely terrace and watch the soft lights paint the distant villa-dotted hills, in mellow shades of gold.

There are a couple of towns which are worth seeing before leaving the Asolo area.   If brandy holds a special interest for you, BASSANO DEL GRAPPA is an old town famous for its production of grappa (or brandy).   The town is also a pottery center.   However, it is rather large, and in my estimation, much less interesting than a tiny town just a few miles further on, MAROSTICA.   If you are in this area in September, I would suggest that you check on dates and consider a stop in Marostica because on the first Sunday in September - in alternate years - the central square is transformed into a giant chess board and local citizens become the human chess pieces.   Even if it isn't the year of the chess game, Marostica is a cute little medieval town encircled by walls whose delightful little central square is surrounded by colorful buildings with a castle forming one side.   There is also a second castle guarding the town from the top of the hill.

As you head north into the Dolomites there are various routes to choose from. The major highway heads north through Feltre and Belluno and then on to Cortina.   However, if the day is nice and your spirit of adventure is high, there is really nothing more fun than the "back roads" through the mountains.   The Michelin maps are a great aid in this respect because they mark in green various small roads which are particularly scenic, and as you head north you can experiment with these choices and your journey should take you through tiny hamlets and gorgeous mountain valleys far from the normal tourist path.

You might want to be loose and just choose your own little country inn in one of the lovely little valleys of the Dolomites, but if you are making reservations, I would suggest an overnight in CORTINA D' AMPEZZO.   This is not a little town.   In fact, it has grown into a large tourist center due to its excellent skiing facilities; however, the location is truly superb with gigantic granite peaks ringing the town.   In Cortina there are many hotels.   I prefer one with a history that dates far before the skiing craze, the MENARDI.   According to the charming owner, Angelo Menardi, the inn was originally a peasant home - in his family for one hundred and fifty years.   Gradually the farm house became an inn giving shelter to those seeking a bed for the night - more often than not in the hay loft!   Times have changed and today the Mendari is a proper hotel where the guests sleep in beds with down comforters and all the guest rooms have private baths.   However, much of the original atmosphere remains with marvelous antiques cleverly incorporated into the decor.   Great taste and the warmth of the gracious owners exudes in every detail.   The Mendari was originally a farm house, but civilization has crept in and today the inn is located on the north side of Cortina directly on the main highway heading toward Toblach.

Hotel Menardi
Cortina

When it is time to leave Cortina for further mountain adventures you will be taking the Old Dolomite Road heading west from Cortina to Bolzano. This historic pass was originally used by the merchants of Venice on their way to Germany. Follow the highway S48 from Cortina which will take you over a wind swept barren pass surrounded by towering granite peaks. The road then drops into a valley before climbing again to conquer the Pordoi Pass and then down into the Fassa Valley. When you reach the town of Vigo di Fassa leave the road you are on and head west over the Carezza Pass. Along the way on your left you will pass Lake Carezza which although small is certainly worth a stop to savour this delightful green lake surrounded by mountain peaks. Soon after leaving Lake Carezza you arrive in the town of Nova Levante.

The route from Cortina to Nova Levante is well marked, but from this town on you will need to watch for the road signs. Just a few miles beyond Nova Levante you will come to a junction. At this intersection take the road to the left and keeping to the left follow the signs for EGA, EGGEN, OBEREGGEN, or SAN FLORIANO. In this part of Italy the town names are most confusing because each town is named both in Italian and also in the old Austrian name since before the first world war this section of Italy belonged to the Austrian Empire. So, Ega and Eggen are the same town, and Obereggen and San Floriano are the same town. Your hotel, the HOTEL BEWALLERHOF, is located between these two tiny hamlets. It sounds complicated to find. It is. You will probably get lost along the way, after leaving Nova Levante, but just stop and ask directions and make certain you have a detailed map. (The best ones, which you will be able to find in Cortina, are the VERY detailed hiking path maps which also have the highways indicated.) If the weather is clear this route from Cortina to Obereggen will take you through some of the most glorious mountains in the world, and when you reach your final destination, you will find yourself in one of the really special "hideaways" in the world! The Hotel Bewallerhof is truly idyllic. Whereas, your last hotel was in the bustling town of Cortina, the Bewallerhof is almost as isolated as it can be. Leaving the town of Ega (or Eggen) you will soon see a sign on the left of the road saying "Bewallerhof." Turning left you weave through a pine forest which then opens into a meadow crowned by an old farm house, complete with barn and cows! This is your hotel. And what a site! The deck in the front of the hotel has a panoramic view which stretches for miles over meadows which sweep down to rows of mountains. Behind the hotel the granite peaks of the Dolomites rise dramatically in the sky forming a majestic natural backdrop to the farmhouse. For some tastes this hotel will be too isolated. For some personalities the hotel will be too simple. But, you will definitely not be "roughing it ", all the rooms have private baths and the decor is simple but very inviting with light wooden furniture, plants, and lots of paneling. The emphasis is on the out of doors. What bliss to walk for miles in any direction surrounded by such beauty!

Hotel Bewallerhof
   Obereggen

If you are a mountain enthusiast you might just decide to stay forever at the Hotel Bewallerhof, but when it is time to continue on, be consoled by the fact that there is another magnificent hotel awaiting at the end of your day's journey and a wonderful town to visit enroute.

When you depart from Obereggen return to the main road, marked S241, and follow the splendid Val d'Ega (Ega Valley) as it weaves its way through a dramatic gorge.   The road joins the main expressway just north of Bolzano where I recommend taking the expressway north to BRESSANONE.   Try to time your stop at Bressanone for lunch because this small city has much to offer. It is a walled medieval town ringed by mountains.   There is a charming little village square plus a river - lined on both banks by promenades - meandering through the center.   Bressanone hides another treasure, the ELEFANT!   This inn is famous for its exquisite cuisine.   In its beautiful dining rooms only the freshest foods and wines are served - usually from the hotel's own farms and vineyards.   But the hotel also has an intriguing tale.   In the sixteenth century an elephant was being delivered to Maximilian of Austria as a special gift. Well, it seems this "gift" grew weary of walking by the time it arrived in Bressanone and so was housed at the local inn - you guessed it - the Elefant. The story alone merits a stop, but the joy is that the Elefant also retains so much character and serves such excellent food.

From Bressanone you can take the expressway north toward the Brenner Pass, soon leaving the expressway near Vipiteno to head south west along a twisting road which maneuvers the Monte Giovo Pass as it twists its way through the mountains and then drops down into the valley to follow the Passiria river as it winds a path into Merano.

NOTE: If your destination is Austria, then at Vipiteno continue north on the expressway for the short drive to the Brenner Pass leading into Austria.

In MERANO I suggest the CASTEL FREIBERG, an enchanting fairytale castle on a knoll of a hill dominating the countryside with its majesty. This fabulous castle has everything - setting, view, marvelous architecture, gourmet food, beautiful rooms, priceless antiques, pool, tennis, and friendly, professional management.

Castel Frieberg
Merano

DESTINATION V   GARGNANO   Pensione Baia D'Oro

It is a short drive south from Merano to Bolzano where you will meet the freeway heading toward Trent which in the 16th century is the town where the Catholic council met to establish important articles of faith which emphasized the authority of the Catholic church.

Leave the freeway at Trent and head west toward the small, but lovely green LAKE TOBLINO which is enhanced by a superb castle on its north shore where you can stop for lunch. From Toblino there is a beautiful country road lined with fruit trees and vineyards which heads directly south to Lake Garda, Italy's largest lake. On the northern shore of Lake Garda is the town of RIVA. Although the town has grown with the construction of modern facilities to accommodate the tourists, there is still a nucleus forming the Old Town of Riva near the harbor where you will find the Piazza III Novembre and the Tower of Apponale which dates from the 13th century.

Leaving Riva take the road along the western shoreline. It is a kaleidoscope of vistas as the road weaves through seventy tunnels and over fifty-six bridges snaking its way along the cliffs. Each tunnel holds a new surprise as you emerge to view the lake from a fresh perspective.

Pensione Baia D'Oro
Gargnano

You pass through several small villages before arriving at VILLA DI GARGNANO where, located directly on the lake, is a very simple, but cozy pensione, the BAIA D'ORO.   As you enter there is a bar to the right and an intimate lounge to the left.   Beyond is a dining room which is noted for its its excellent Italian cuisine.   The walls of the dining room are decorated with the paintings of Gianbattista Terzi, an Italian artist who has had exhibitions at many of the art museums of Italy.   It just so happens that the Terzi family owns this tiny hotel which accounts for the art display!   The dining room opens onto a delightful terrace strategically perched over Lake Garda where guests can soak in the sun while enjoying the action on the lake.

The town of Gargnano is an excellent choice for a lake interlude due to its central location which lends itself beautifully to exploring by hydrofoil or steamer the delightful villages which hug the shore of the lake.   If you have the time, I would choose a different destination each day - perhaps planning to have a bite of lunch at an appealing little lakeside cafe.   However, if you only have time for one adventure, I recommend taking a ferry or hydrofoil to the scenic town of SIRMIONE, a wonderful walled village at the south end of Lake Garda positioned at the end of a miniature peninsula which proudly pokes it head into the lake.   During the summer this town is absolutely bursting with tourists. But you can certainly understand.   This is another one of Italy's "stage setting" villages, almost too perfect to be true.   If you take the ferry or hydrofoil to Sirmione your boat will dock in the center of the town and you can stroll through the little boutiques, perhaps have a bite of lunch at one of the beautiful terrace cafes overlooking the lake, and explore the tiny island-like village.   Sirmione is definitely one of Europe's most picturesque villages.   (Note: if you would prefer a larger, more deluxe hotel than the simple Baia D'Oro, in Sirmione there is an elegant alternative, the Villa Cortine Palace which is described in the hotel section at the back of the book.)

In addition to the marvelous lake excursions, while at Gargnano you might want to visit a museum nearby, the VITTORIALE, once the home of Gabriele D'Annunzio, the celebrated Italian poet.   (For those of us who love stories of romance, D'Annunzio is also famous for his love affair with Eleanora Duse.)

It might be easier to leave the Pensione Baia D'Oro knowing that the GRAND HOTEL VILLA SERBELLONI on Lake Como awaits your arrival.   The Villa Serbolloni will be a nice contrast because although both are lake front, the Baia D'Oro is intimate and tiny whereas the Villa Serbelloni is large and imposing.

On your way from your villa on Lake Garda to your villa on Lake Como, I highly suggest making one stop.   You will pass through a fabulous town which should not be missed, BERGAMO, only about an hour's drive west of Gardone.   As you approach Bergamo it will not look worth a stop - but it is!   The shell of the city is deceiving because it hides a lovely kernel, the CITA ALTA, or high city. The lower part of Bergamo is modern and pleasant, but the old medieval city snuggled on the top of the hill holds such treasures as the Piazza Vecchia, the Colleoni Chapel, and the Church of St. Mary Major.   Should you want to time your stop in Bergamo with lunch, there are several excellent restaurants.   A delicious family style meal can be had at the Agnello d"Oro, a cozy charming l7th century inn in the Citta Alta.

From Bergamo it is a short drive on to BELLAGIO, a medieval town located at the tip of a peninsula dividing the lower section of Lake Como into two lakes, Lake Como on the west and Lake Lecco on the east. In this town with gates opening onto the main square is your hotel, the GRAND HOTEL VILLA SERBELLONI, a large imposing old world style palace hotel offering everything you could wish for in a lakeside interlude - tennis, swimming pool, boat excursions, private beach, and more.   The hotel is very ornate, still retaining its glory of bygone days.   In fact the hotel is almost overwhelming with its soaring ceilings intricately painted, heavy chandeliers, and a fabulous sweeping staircase.   The setting of the Villa Serbolloni is superb and overshadows what might be perceived as a slighty "faded elegance" of the hotel's decor.

Just a few steps from the hotel lies the charming little town of Bellagio where you can meander through the medieval village or walk to the pier for one of the boats which will take you to all corners of the lake. What a wonderful excursion! Lake Como is absolutely beautiful - especially the lower eastern branch of the lake called Lake Lecco where cliffs enclose the shorelines like gorgeous walls and give a fjord-like beauty to the area. There are numerous romantic steamers which glide in and out of the picturesque, softly hued little hamlets dotting the lake shore. You can settle onto a steamer equipped with bar and restaurant and from your armchair lazily enjoy the constantly changing, but always intriguing shoreline as the boat maneuvers in and out of the colorful little harbors, past elegant private villas, by postcard pretty villages. From Bellagio you can also step on board one of the swift hydrofoils which will whisk you about the lake. Or, from Bellagio you can put your car right on the ferry to either Cadenabbia on the western shore of Lake Como or Varenna on the eastern shore of the lake. In any case, this lake is not to be missed.

Grand Hotel Villa Serbelloni
Bellagio

With Bellagio as a base there are several several sightseeing possibilities. An excursion to visit the VILLA CARLOTTA, a fairy tale like 18th century palace - worthy of the Prussian Princess Carlotta for whom it was named - is enjoyable. My suggestion would be to take the car ferry from Bellagio to Cadenabbia on the western shore. From there it is just a short drive along the beautiful tree lined Via del Paradiso to the Villa Carlotta which is encircled by its own gorgeous park of terraced gardens.

DESTINATION VII   ISOLA DEI PESCATORI   Hotel Verbano

DEVIATION NOTE: Should your plans call for ending your Italian sojourn and heading on into Switzerland this would be an excellent point to begin your journey.   Head north along Lake Como and on to Chiavenna where you then turn east for the short drive (only about 6 miles) to the Swiss border.   From there it is a lovely drive through the Engadine Valley to St. Moritz.

Continuing on toward LAKE MAGGIORE, take advantage of the expressways to make your drive as easy as possible because there is usually heavy traffic in this part of Italy.   It is best to head directly south from Bellagio to pick up the freeway in the direction of Milan.   Keep on the bypass which skirts to the north of Milan and follow the freeway northwest to Lake Maggiore.   When you reach the lake continue along the western shore to STRESA.

It seems only suitable that for a "Mountain and Lake Adventure" one of your hotels should be located on an island in the lake - so we have chosen for you one of the Borromean Islands, ISOLA DEI PESCATORI (Fisherman's Island), located in Lake Maggiore.   This is an enchanting little island with twisting narrow alley-like streets and colorful fishermen's cottages.   As the name implies, this is still an active fishing village. During the tourist season the island teams with people and the streets are lined with rather tacky souvenir shops, but it is hard to dull the charm of this quaint town.

Hotel Verbano
Isola dei Pescatori

This island can be reached by ferry from Stressa, Baveno, or Pallanza, but the most popular of these is Stressa from which there are frequent departures by boat to Isola dei Pescatori. Your hotel, the VERBANO, is definitely not a deluxe hotel. In fact, it would not be suitable for those who only enjoy fancy hotels because this is a small, very simple, very basic hotel. The lobby is quite plain. The bedrooms too are very simple. However, if you appreciate all kinds of hotels for the special attributes they have to offer, I think you will love the Verbano. It has a delightful terrace with dining tables set overlooking the lake, the bedrooms too have beautiful vistas and some even offer large patios. The food is delicious (the same cook for twenty-eight years!), and the service of the Faachera family, who own and personally manage the Verbano, is warm and gracious.

This tiny archipelago consisting of Isola Bella (Beautiful Island), Isola dei Pescatori (Fisherman's Island), and Isola Madre (Mother Island) are world famous for their dramatic palaces and spectacular, fragrant gardens. How smug you will be to settle into your room then have a drink on the lovely terrace and watch the last of the tourists hustle onto the boat for shore, leaving you to enjoy the sunset.

DESTINATION VIII   CHAMPOLUC   Anna Maria

DEVIATION NOTE: Should your next destination be Zermatt, then it is time to leave Italy by heading north to Domodossolo.   About ten miles beyond Domodossolo you arrive at Iselle where you drive your car piggy back style onto the train and ride in your car as you zig zag through the fabulous Simplon Tunnel and emerge about twenty minutes later in Brig, Switzerland.

From Orta drive south to the main freeway and head west toward Turin.   Before reaching Turin watch for the signs and take the branch of the expressway heading toward Aosta.   When you come to Verres, leave the highway and take the small road north to CHAMPOLUC.   The road follows the Evancon River as it cuts its path through the mountains.   At first the valley is quite steep and narrow and then opens up into wide meadows lazily stretching out on both sides of the river. In early summer the meadows are truly lovely blanketed in brilliantly colored wild flowers.   The drive from the expressway is an hour to Champoluc.

Just before the road leaves Champoluc you will see a marker for the ANNA MARIA HOTEL.   At this sign turn to the right and follow the road for a very short drive up the hill until you see the hotel.   It is beautifully located amid the pine trees and has views in every direction of the spectacular mountains.   The

Anna Maria is a charming small chalet style inn owned and managed by the gracious and efficient Anna Maria. The dining room is cozy and inviting with gay red checked curtains at the windows and rustic Alpine style carved wooden chairs. The bedrooms although small all have private bathrooms and are most appealing with panelled walls and a country flavor.

Anna Maria
Champoluc

When it is time to leave Champoluc you have two options if you want to travel into Switzerland. First you must drive back to the main expressway and head west. In about a half hour you will come to Aosta at which point you can leave the expressway for the road leading north to the San Bernardo tunnel and into Switzerland's Rhone Valley. Or by continuing on the expressway west through the village of Courmayeur, you arrive at the Mont Blanc tunnel which delivers you briefly into France, but within a hour more to Geneva by a main highway. Of course, by taking the short drive to Milan you can easily "tie in" with another Italian holiday suggested in this guide.

Romantic Hilltowns of Tuscany & Umbria

FLORENCE

PANZANO
IN CHIANTI

Arezzo

San Gimignano   Siena   *Cortona*

SINALUNGA

Abbey of Monte
Oliveto Maggiore   Pienza   *Ferugia*   ASSISI

Torgiano

Spoleto
Monteluco

ORVIETO
Todi

•ROME

ROMANTIC HILLTOWNS OF TUSCANY & UMBRIA

Nothing could possibly surpass the exquisite beauty of the countryside near Florence in the Spring. It is absolutely breathtaking! Actually, any time of the year, if you meander into the hill towns south of Florence, all your senses will be rewarded with the splendors that this enchanting Italian countryside has to offer. Almost every hillock is crowned with a picture-perfect little walled village. The fields are brilliant with vibrant red poppies. The vineyards lace the fields in all their glory and promise. The dusky grey-green of the olive trees dress the hillsides. Pine forests unexpectedly appear to highlight the landscape. As if this were not enough, this area secretes within her little villages and countryside retreats some of the finest small hotels in all the world. And if this is still not sufficient to tempt you away from the normal tourist route, be reminded that the food and wines are superb.

So, when you plan your trip to Italy, please allow time to treat yourself to a unique adventure. Save at least a few days to slip away from the cities and into the countryside. Perhaps you will not have time to follow this entire itinerary, but at least sneak in a few days in this magnificent area. You will be well rewarded with a wealth of memories which will linger long after you return home.

ORIGINATING CITY   FLORENCE

Your journey begins in Florence. Allow enough time to savour this marvelous city but, if you are reluctant to leave, be consoled. There are magnificent treats in store for you in the delightful hill towns which surround Florence. Great art was not confined within the city limits of Florence and you will see magnificent cathedrals and beautiful works of art throughout the neighboring areas. Yet the real treats in store for you are not only the masterpieces made by man, but also those made by God.

1ST DESTINATION   ASSISI   Hotel Subasio

The traffic around Florence is difficult, so quickly find the expressway to Rome and follow it until you come to the turnoff for Arezzo, which is located about six miles east of the highway. You might want to bypass Arezzo. Although it is a medieval town with a rich history dating back to the Etruscan Era, it is a large city and it is not as quaint as some of its smaller neighbors.

If you follow the main road south from Arezzo, you will soon arrive at CORTONA. This is a beautifully situated, walled town climbing up a steep hillside covered with olive trees. Stop to enjoy the atmosphere of this medieval town with its crazy little twisting streets, jumble of small squares and colorful buildings. A mighty castle dramatically stands guard over this hillside town.

Leaving Cortona, continue south to Lake Trasimeno and follow along the northern shore on to PERUGIA, a large medieval city encompassed by ramparts. An important Umbrian city since Etruscan days, the heart of the old city is the Piazza IV Novembre, a beautiful square with an especially appealing fountain, the Fontana Maggiore, built in the late 13th century.

It is only a short drive further south from Perugia to ASSISI. Even if it were not for the lingering warmth of the gentle St. Francis, this would be a delightful borough. In fact, I think it is one of the most spectacular of all the hill towns in Umbria. Perhaps there are a few too many souvenir shops, but this is a small price to pay for such a very special place. The town walls begin on the lower slopes of the valley and perfectly enclose the area as it climbs the steep hillside with a climax in an enormous crowning castle. Assisi is a marvelous town for walking; you will need sturdy shoes to wind your way up and down the puzzle of tiny streets. It is great fun. You will come across intriguing little lanes which open into small squares. When you stop to rest, there will be marvelous vistas of the breathtaking Umbrian fields stretching out below. There is the fabulous St. Francis' Basilica which includes a monastery with a beautiful arcaded courtyard.

To savour the beauty of Assisi, it is fun to spend the night and, luckily, there are several excellent hotel choices. Beautifully situated with one of its walls forming a section of the piazza of the St. Francis' Basilica is the HOTEL SUBASIO. This is not a deluxe hotel but it has much to entice the tourist. Perhaps its most splendid attribute is the view. From the vine covered dining terraces, there are splendid views of the glorious undulating Umbrian fields; these seem to glow with a special radiance. Some of the bedrooms, too, have gorgeous views from their balconies. Definitely splurge and request one of the best rooms so you can capture each possible moment of this very beautiful scene.

While staying at Assisi, drive one day the short distance to TORGIANO where there is a splendid wine museum. One would never dream that such a tiny town could boast such a stunning museum, but it is not a coincidence. The Lungarotti family owns the vineyards for miles in every direction and, indeed, they must be a very clever and dedicated family. They also own a delightful hotel in the center of town, LE TRE VASELLE. In addition to overseeing the decoration of this exquisite hotel, the Signore Lungarotti also collected artifacts pertaining to every aspect of the production of wine from the earliest days which are in the museum. The collection is spectacular, worthy of a detour by anyone interested in wines. Not only is the museum delightful but the collection is so beautifully displayed that it is a joy to visit.

Hotel Subasio
Assisi

Although only a short drive from Assisi to Orvieto by the direct route, a sightseeing excursion is worthwhile.   If you drive south from Assisi you will soon come to SPOLETO.   This is a very interesting town.   Not only is this another of the beautifully preserved medieval cities with a dramatic hilltop location, but it also has an almost unbelievable bridge.   Dating from the Roman days, it spans the deep ravine between Spoleto and the adjoining mountain. It is almost inconceivable that such a bridge could have been built over a Roman aqueduct existing in the 14th century.   The bridge is 755 feet long and 262 feet high!   It is supported by a series of ten Gothic arches and has a fort at the far end as well as a balcony in the center!

Before leaving the vicinity of Spoleto, if you are a St. Francis enthusiast, you certainly must make the short detour to visit MONTELUCO, where St. Francis came to live as a hermit.   You will appreciate why he chose Monteluco after you twist to the top of the mountain and enjoy the glorious view of the surrounding hillsides covered with olive trees.

If you have not had your fill of walled villages, you might enjoy a brief stop, as you head west, at TODI, another of the tiny hilltop walled villages about midway between Spoleto and Orvieto.   However, do not linger too long in Todi because Orvieto is a real prize.

ORVIETO is spread across the top of a hill which drops down on every side in steep volcanic cliffs.   One wonders how the town could ever have been built! At Orvieto's center is a glorious duomo dominating a beautiful piazza.   You may think you have seen enough stunning cathedrals, but this one is really special - brilliantly colored in intricate mosaic designs and accentuated by slender spirals stretching gracefully into the sky.

Also of great interest in Orvieto is the visit to another engineering feat, St. Patrick's Well. This well, over 200 feet deep, was hewn out of solid volcanic rock to collect and store water in case of a siege.

Your hotel for tonight's stay is not in the town of Orvieto but just a short drive to the south at LA BADIA, a sightseeing event in its own right. The hotel is built within the ruins of an ancient abbey. The hotel has a castle-like ambiance with high vaulted ceilings and cozy nooks. Request one of the rooms with a view up to the town of Orvieto where you can admire the beautiful duomo cresting the top of the hill. La Badia also has a large pool which is a delightful addition at the end of a long summer day.

La Badia
Orvieto

Since your distance is so short between Orvieto and Sinalunga, instead of taking one of the major highways, explore the small back roads, winding through the countryside as you head north. As a goal, mark on the map the small town of PIENAZA as your first target. It does not matter if you get a little lost. The scenery is beautiful and you will probably discover your own little walled village. One of my favorites is the marvelous small town of Pienza. It is just lovely. It has a pristine beauty and has no modern developments to interrupt the charm of this tiny town, surrounded by walls which cap the hilltop. Within the town you will find quaint little squares and a church built almost on the edge of the ramparts with a lovely terrace view. A few miles north of Pienza is the Abbey of Monte Oliveto Maggiore. Of special interest are the terracottas adorning the entrance, created by the famous artist, Luca della Robbia. The abbey is serenely situated among the cypress forest. The cloisters contain frescoes portraying the life of St. Benedict.

Locanda dell'Amorosa
Sinalunga

From the Abbey, drive east to the town of SINALUNGA where there is a very delightful hotel, the LOCANDA DELL' AMOROSA. This hotel, in addition to being a wonderful place to spend the night, is really a sightseeing experience. The road to the Locanda dell' Amorosa is lined on both sides with tall Cypress trees through which you glimpse an expanse of vineyards. The town walls are actually the hotel's entrance, as the hotel is the town. Pass through the gate into a large courtyard and at its end is an exquisite little church. The wing of buildings to the left contain the bedrooms. The wing to the right houses the reception lounge and the dining room. In this same little "hotel-town" a delicious wine is bottled which you can sample at dinner. I know you will enjoy your stay here.

DESTINATION IV   PANZANO IN CHIANTI   Villa le Barone

On your way to Panzano be sure to stop in SIENA. This is a delightful city and deserves many hours to savour all its attributes. The village is another of the strategically built walled hill towns. The ramparts are perfectly preserved with massive gates guarding a meticulously maintained medieval stronghold. Drive as close as you can to the main square and park your car. All the sightseeing can and should be done by foot. The giant piazza is a sight in itself. It is immense and instead of being square, is fan shaped. All the streets surrounding the square end like the spokes of a giant wheel in the Piazza del Campo. The town hall monopolizes one side of the piazza with graceful arches embellished with the coat of arms of Siena. It is in this gigantic piazza where the colorful "Palio delle Contrade" takes place in July and August every year. The horse race is only a part of this colorful spectacle of medieval costumes, wonderful banners and parades. You can check for the exact dates, but the festivities extend beyond the actual date of the races. Also, Siena has one of

Italy's most dramatic cathedrals, located a short walk from the Piazza del Campo.   Not only is the cathedral   striking - with its bold patterns of black and white marble - but it also houses a marvelous museum.

From Siena, continue north on the expressway and take the turnoff for SAN GIMIGNANO.   Although you might think you are weary of walled towns, San Gimignano is quite unique and definitely worth a stop.   What is so dramatic about San Gimignano is that at one time this small walled village was surrounded by seventy-two towers!   During the Middle Ages it was a status symbol for noble families to each build personal towers for protection.   The higher the tower the greater the image of wealth and importance.   It is amazing that four-teen of the original towers of San Gimignano are still standing.   They make a striking silhouette soaring like skyscrapers against the sky.   On a clear day, you can see them on the horizon from miles away.   In addition to the romance of the towers, San Gimignano is a charming medieval village and there is an excellent restaurant (also a delightful hotel), LA CISTERNA, found on the main square.

From San Gimingano, head almost directly east to PANZANO IN CHIANTI where the prize of your journey, VILLA LE BARONE, awaits you.   This is an exquisite small hotel encompassing all the joys that are Tuscany.   This lovely villa was once the home of the Della Robbia family.   Today it is owned by the Duchess Visconti.   The location is idyllic.   The villa is set in lovely gardens and surrounded by vineyards.   There is a welcoming pool.   A terrace for dining overlooks a panorama of the Tuscany hills stretching for miles in the distance. Another dining room is fashioned from the former stables.   Breakfast and din-ner are included in the price and reservations during the high season are usually only accepted for a stay of several days; but this is no problem...you will want to stay forever!

When it is time to complete your loop and return to Florence you will find it only about an hour's drive away in time but years away in mood from the tranquility of the Villa le Barone.

Villa le Barone
Panzano

Rome to Milan
via the Italian Riviera

MILAN
Pavia Carthusian
Monastery

Genoa
Camogli
PORTOFINO
Cinque Terre
La Spezia
Carrara
LUCCA
FLORENCE
Pisa

SWITZERLAND

AUSTRIA

FRANCE

ROME

ROME TO MILAN VIA THE ITALIAN RIVIERA

This itinerary includes one of the most picturesque jewels of Italy - the Italian Riviera where not only are there charming towns snuggled into small coves along the shoreline, but also the road itself is a masterpiece of engineering. The coastal highway along the Riviera "bridges" for miles - high in the sky above the ravines, and "tunnels" in and out of the cliffs rising steeply from the sea. The original title for this itinerary was "Coastal Route from Rome to Milan", but after personally experiencing the drive, the route and the name were changed. There is an expressway partially following the coast from Rome to Pisa, but until this is finished the road is one of total frustration with a solid line of trucks and cars making the journey undesirable. Far easier, and actually more scenic, is to take the expressway north from Rome to Florence through the gorgeous Tuscany hills then to head west on to Pisa and finally travel on via the coast to Genoa and Milan. It is impossible to include all of the towns that dot the coastline, but after ducking on and off the freeway ourselves, we have tried to include some of the most charming and colorful.

70   Rome to Milan via the Italian Riviera

ORIGINATING CITY   ROME

This itinerary begins in Rome, a favorite of all and a wonderful introduction to Italy.   In the hotel section there are many suggestions for accommodations to suit your taste and budget.   When you are saturated with the overwhelming sights that Rome has to offer and are ready to continue your journey, buy an excellent map to assist you in maneuvering out of the city and onto the magnificent expressway heading north.

DESTINATION I   LUCCA   Villa la Princepessa

This itinerary assumes that you have already visited Florence, certainly one of the highlights of any Italian holiday.   If not, you will certainly want to stop in Florence for several days.   Otherwise when the expressway from Rome reaches Florence, take the major branch to the west and continue on toward PISA.   You will probably want to stop in Pisa for a few pictures of her Leaning Tower, but frankly I consider Pisa overrated.   It is such a solid mass of tourists and souvenir shops during the summer season that you can hardly find a place to park before trying to squirm your way to the central piazza.   I must admit that the duomo, gleaming white with its companion leaning tower, is impressive, so if you have never seen it, do stop.   But even more interesting and not nearly so "touristy" is the beautiful city of LUCCA located only a few miles to the north. This too is an ancient city, even more perfectly preserved than its neighbor, Pisa.   Lucca has surrounding the city an enormous wall so wide that that it even harbors delightful small parks and a road which runs along the top.   A drive along the top of these ramparts is a wonderful way to get a bird's eye view of this extremely picturesque medieval town before you park your car and explore on foot.

If you are driving from Pisa to Lucca there is a beautiful villa just to the west of the old road, only a few miles before you come to Lucca. The VILLA LA PRINCEPESSA is a gorgeous palace-style hotel set in a beautiful park with a delightful swimming pool which is a welcome bonus after a long day of sightseeing. The inside of the villa is, in my estimation, somewhat wild in its choice of colors for decor, but the setting is so magnificent and the building so beautiful that I highly recommend it.

Villa La Princepessa
Lucca

DESTINATION II   PORTOFINO   Splendido Hotel

When you leave the Villa La Princepessa, head back to the expressway and continue north. What looks like glaciers soon shimmer white in the foothills of the

Apuan Alps which rise to the right of the highway. This is not snow at all, but rather your introduction to the beautiful white Italian marble. You might enjoy a detour from the highway for the short drive into the hills to the ancient town of CARRARA - famous through the ages for its marvelous white marble. As you wander this historic old town you will be following the footsteps of the perfectionist, Michelangelo, who used to personally come to Carrara to choose huge blocks of marble from which to carve his masterpieces.

Leaving Carrara you will enjoy an adventure of an entirely different kind - exploring the five little isolated towns on the coast called CINQUE TERRE. This area is quickly becoming linked with civilization so if you love the thrill of discovering old fishing villages still untouched by time do not tarry.

To begin this portion of your journey take the small road from Carrara west returning to the main highway and continuing on to the port of LA SPEZIA, a large sea port and navy town. From here you might want to take the short drive to the tip of the peninsula south of Spezia to visit the old fishing village of PORTOVERERE - which clings to the steep rocks rising from the sea. This was one of Lord Byron's haunts when he lived across the bay at San Terenzo. You will then need to return to La Spezia to continue your journey.

The Cinque Terre used to be five completely isolated fishing villages on a stretch of land between La Spezia to the south and Levanto to the north. First only a footpath connected these hamlets, then a train was installed, and now real civilization is encroaching with a road under construction which will open them all to the world of tourism. Three of the towns are accessible now by road. From La Spezia you can travel to RIOMAGGIORE and then on to MANOROLA. From the northern approach of Levanto you can travel by road to the first town of MONTEROSSO. Still completely cut off from car traffic are the ancient fishing hamlets between - VARNAZZA and CORNIGLIA. It is best to drive as far as possible from La Spazia stopping first at Riomaggiore and then on to Manorola. Upon arrival you can let your mood, the time, and the weather dictate your explorations.   You can continue on by hiking the spectacular trails connecting the villages, by taking the small ferry between them, by using the train - or best yet, combine them all!   If you have time to see only one of the scenic towns, Vernazza, which clings perilously to a rocky promontory forming a tiny harbor, is perhaps the most scenic.

After Cinque Terre continue north along the coast.   If you are in a hurry return to the freeway A 12.   If time is not a problem, continue along the coast via the towns of SESTRI LEVANTE and CHIAVARI to SAN MARGHERITA.   Here you take the small road south for the short drive to the "picture book" village of PORTOFINO.   This last section of the road, especially in summer, is jammed with traffic, but the plum at the end is worth the hassle.   Portofino certainly has   already been discovered but it is so delightful it deserves its accolades.

Hotel Splendido
Portofino

As you approach Portofino watch for the entrance sign for the SPLENDIDO HOTEL.   There is a guard at the entrance and only those with reservations are allowed to follow the little road as it winds up the hill to the magnificent villa style hotel.   The Splendido is a deluxe hotel.   A very expensive hotel whose prices include breakfast and dinner.   But what a gorgeous setting!   The hotel is perched in the hills above the town with splendid views of the sea and the harbor. A beautiful swimming pool nestles below the hotel and tennis courts are found in the gardens to the left.   There are enchanting little trails threading their way throughout the gardens which surround the hotel.   Along the paths benches are strategically positioned for quiet moments to savour the stunning view.   It is an easy walk into Portofino if you can bear to leave your oasis.

Portofino is considered a national treasure and it truly is a jewel.   Her tiny harbor is filled with gorgeous yachts, small ferries, and colorful fishing boats.   In the center of town is a delightful small square.   Enveloping the harbor are colorful tall and narrow fishermen's cottages painted in warm colors of siennas, ochres, and pinks with green shutters.   Bright flower boxes accent the windows and the laundry flaps gaily in the breeze.   Vivid reflections of these quaint little houses shimmer in the emerald water.   Beyond the town the heavily forested, beautiful green hills rise steeply to complete this idyllic scene.

DESTINATION V   MILAN   Marino alla Scala

DEVIATION NOTE: For those of you travelling to the French Riviera, we wish you "adieu" in Portofino.   From there you will continue to follow the coastal highway west to Genoa along the Italian Riviera into France, to the French Riviera and across to the principality of Monaco.

For the rest of "our group", after leaving Portofino return to the main highway and continue west for about eighteen miles to Genoa.   Bypass Genoa and instead, as you circle the city watch for the freeway to the north going to Milan.

An enjoyable detour on your way north is the PAVIA CARTHUSIAN MONASTERY (Certosa di Pavia).   Probably the simplest way to find it would be to watch for the turn off to Pavia (about sixty miles north of Genoa).   At this point take the road east to Pavia and from there go north about five miles to the Carthusian Monastery.   Lavishly built in the 15th century this splendid monastery is claimed by some to be one of the finest buildings in Italy. (Check carefully the days and hours open - it is usually closed on Mondays and for several hours mid day).   The outside of the monastery is lavishly designed with colorful marble and intricate designs.   Inside, the small cloisters are especially charming with one hundred twenty-two arches framed by beautiful terra cotta moldings. There is also a baroque fountain within plus several small gardens.   Next to the monastery the Palace of the Dukes of Milan has been turned into a museum.

Marino alla Scala
Milan

After your tour of the monastery it is approximately sixteen miles further north to Milan.   Milan has many large commercial hotels, but if you enjoy a smaller hotel, consider the MARINO ALLA SCALA, strategically located next to the La Scalla Opera House.   Even if you are not an opera buff, I think you will enjoy this hotel.   When you first enter the reception area or the bedrooms, this hotel may seem a little bland, however it has a very loyal following - the hotel is always full!   The owners do not even need to publish a brochure. Only after you have been there a few days and have enjoyed the excellent service and the impeccably clean rooms will you understand the full charm of this hotel.   Especially endearing is the little bar with its own miniature staircase that leads to a private balcony. The location also is absolutely terrific.   You are only steps from the opera house, but also only a half block to the splendid glass domed shopping arcade, lined with beautiful boutiques and cozy cafes.   After a stroll through the arcade you emerge into an imposing square dominated by a truly spectacular Cathedral, the third largest in the world!   Although Milan is a large sprawling metropolis, her medieval core is delightful and easily explored on foot.

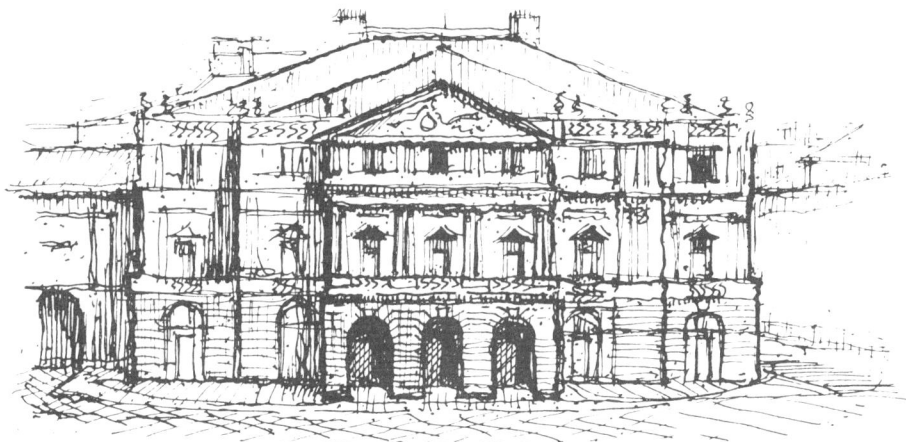

Rome to Milan via the Italian Riviera   77

Rome

Anzio
Nettuno

Abbey of
Monte Cassino

Dubrovnik

Corfu & Greece

Naples Pompei RAVELLO
Salerno

Bari Castellana Caves
ALBEROBELLO

Capri

Paestum

Potenza
Matera Taranto Brindisi

Highlights
of Southern Italy
& Sicily

Sibari

TROPEA

Erice PALERMO Messina
Trapani Villa San Giovanni
Marsala Segesta Cefalu
Selinunte Enna TAORMINA
Agrigento Piazza Catania
Armerina Siracuse

Suggested Side Trips

HIGHLIGHTS OF SOUTHERN ITALY & SICILY

Having visited the famous trio of Rome, Florence, and Venice, most tourists think that they have "seen" Italy. If childhood geography lessons call forth such names as Pompei, Herculaneum and Paestum, all too frequently the urge to visit these jewels of archaeoligical wonders is lost in the misconception that Southern Italy is an uninteresting destination. What a waste! Southern Italy has fascinating ruins, gorgeous coastlines, beautiful medieval walled villages, lovely beaches, marvelous hilltowns, and some of the most unusual sights in Italy. Best yet, what fun to return home and casually mention to your dinner partner, who thinks he has been everywhere, that you think the Emerald Grotto on the Amalfi coast far exceeds the beauty of the Blue Grotto of Capri or that the Greek ruins at Paestum outshine many of those found in Greece or that the mysterious town of Alberobello still haunts you!

Therefore, for those of you who have already seen the fantastic highlights of Northern Italy, we take pleasure in presenting to you the best of Southern Italy. This itinerary makes a circle of Southern Italy in order to suit the travel needs of a wide selection of tourists.   Follow the entire route or select the portion best for you since this itinerary lends itself especially well for the traveler who only wants to take a segment.   As an example, the journey from Rome to Brindisi is a popular one for the lucky tourist on his way to Greece.   Or the west coast is a popular drive for the tourist who wants to visit Sicily and then return to Rome by air or ferry.   And, most popular of all, is the segment from Rome to the Amalfi drive.   So, this itinerary allows you to custom tailor your journey and gives you many wonderful tips on what to see along the way.

ORIGINATING CITY   ROME

Rome is a most convenient starting point to begin a tour of Southern Italy. Rome Airport is the destination of planes from all over the world and here passengers begin their "Roman Holiday".   In Rome one can seep his soul in the wealth of history, art, architecture, museums, and monuments - and build a foundation for the sights which will be encountered on the journey.

Because there is such a wide selection of accommodations in Rome in various price categories and locations, it seems most practical for you to choose the hotel that best suits your personality and budget from the hotel description section in the back of this guide.

Rome always has a monumental traffic problem. Within the city look for strategically located signs that indicate that there is a freeway ahead. It might be quite a distance, but be patient as these signs will lead you to the outskirts of Rome where there is a highway encircling the city. Follow the freeway around to the exit for the major expressway heading south, Highway A2. When you reach this expressway continue south for approximately 80 miles to the exit for CASSINO. Actually you will be able to spot your destination from several miles away because the ABBEY OF MONTE CASSINO crowns the top of a large mountain to the left of the highway as you drive south. When you reach Cassino turn off the expressway and about midway through town the road that winds up the summit of the mountain to the Abbey of Monte Cassino is clearly marked. This abbey is extremely interesting both religiously and historically. In 529 AD the abbey was founded by St. Benedict. For war historians the abbey is also very significant because this is where the Germans held out against the Allied forces for almost a year in World War II. When the mountain was finally conquered in May 1944 it opened the way for Allied forces to move into Rome. As you read your history books it seems strange that one fort could hold out for so long, but when you see the abbey you understand. It is an enormous building on the crest of a precipitous mountain. In the seige the abbey was almost destroyed but it has been rebuilt according to the original plans and is very impressive.

Note: for those of you who for sentimental or historical reasons are especially interested in World War II there is another destination you might well want to visit in this day's journey. ANZIO is a town on the coast about 35 miles south of Rome and could easily be included as a stop before Cassino. It was at Anzio that the British and the Americans landed in January 1944. The emotional reminder of this terrible war is a few miles south at NETTUNO. Here 8,000 white Crosses and Stars of David flow - row after row across the green lawn. There is a circular drive around the park-like grounds which are beautifully maintained. A memorial chapel and small war museum are located at the end of the grounds. For those who lost family or friends during the invasion there is an office to the right as you drive in where you can find out where your loved one is buried.

From Cassino return to the expressway and continue south for about 37 miles until you see the sign for POMPEI. Unless you have absolutely NO interest in archaeology you must stop in Pompei, the city of your childhood geography books, where time was frozen for 25,000 people under the ashes from the eruption of Vesuvius in the year 62. Some of the sites within Pompei are still under repair from the destruction wrought by the mighty 1980 earthquake, but do not let this deter you. There is so much to see that you will never feel cheated by nature's mischief. (If you are REALLY into archaeology you must also visit the NATIONAL ARCHAEOLIGICAL MUSEUM in Naples where many of the artifacts from Pompei are housed in a magnificent museum.)

Time slips back 2,000 years as you wander the streets of Pompei and visit the temples, the lovely homes, the wine shops, bakery, public baths, etc. There is probably no other place where you can feel so strongly the pulse of ancient days. Many of the private homes have been reconstructed so you can marvel at the lovely inner courtyards, beautiful dining rooms in Pompei red with intricate paintings on the walls, fountains, servants quarters, bath rooms, and gardens. At the entrance to Pompei there are souvenir stands where you can purchase a guide book to the city, or if you prefer, you can hire a private guide at the entrance. Pompei is so interesting that you might well want to come back to spend a complete day visiting the city and the nearby ruins of Herculaneum which are also extremely interesting.

Leaving Pompei head to the coast in the direction of Sorrento where the AMALFI DRIVE, which must be one of the most beautiful stretches of coast in the world, begins. Be sure to time your journey when there is sufficient daylight because, not only do you not want to miss any of the vistas, but the road is extremely twisty and precipitous and you will be glad of the best visability.

There are many excellent choices for hotels along the Amalfi drive. Concentrated in just a few miles, are some of the most splendid choices of hotels both budget and luxury in all of Italy. It is hard to recommend just one since each is unique. One of my favorite towns is the cliff clinging village of RAVELLO, reached by a road which twists and winds its way up and up and up and then suddenly delivers you in a little village high in the clouds with absolutely dazzling views.

Hotel Palumbo
Ravello

In Ravello there are several wonderful inns - all of which can be heartily recommended, but none can surpass the delightful PALUMBO. You enter into a lovely light and airy reception room brimming with flowers and sunlight. Tucked throughout the inn are cozy little nooks filled with antiques. The inside dining room is charming, but usually meals are taken outside to enjoy to the maximum the surrounding scenery: steep hills covered with vineyards flowing down to the rugged coast where brilliant blue water dances between the rocks. The garden terrace of the Palumbo is an oasis of beauty and quiet enhanced by spectacular views. On an upper level is still another rooftop terrace where the sun and views are trapped again for the lucky guest. The Palumbo is not a luxury hotel, but what a jewel!

Before leaving Ravello you will certainly want to visit some of the other small fishing villages, which dot the coast, such as POSITANO and AMALFI. These towns during the season are bursting with tourists, but fun to see.

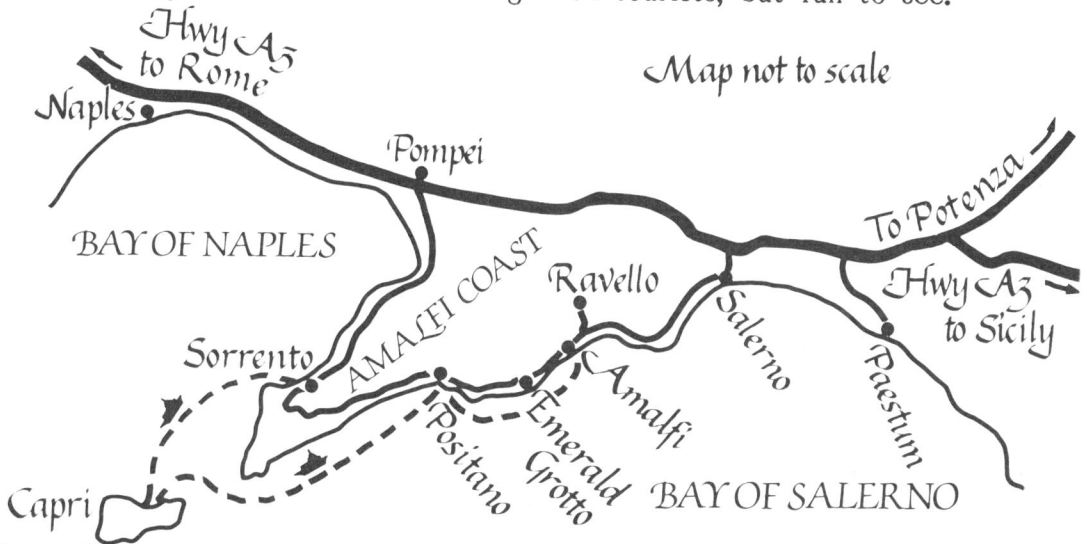

Also, if you have not been able to include an interlude on Capri during your Italian holiday I would suggest an excursion to this enchanted island located just off the coast. Steamers and hydrofoils depart regularly from Sorrento, Amalfi, and Positano. Ask at the tourist bureau or at your hotel for the schedule. (When the seas are rough it is more difficult to leave from Positano since there is no pier and it becomes necessary to take a small boat from the shore to the ferry.)

Also, along the Amalfi coast is the EMERALD GROTTO.   The cave is located between the towns of Amalfi and Positano.   After parking, you buy a ticket and descend by elevator down the steep cliff to a small rocky terrace.   Upon entering the cave which is filled with water, you will be rowed about the grotto in a small boat while your guide explains how the shimmering green water is formed by a secret tunnel allowing sunlight to filter from deep below the surface.   The cave is filled with colorful stalagtites and stalagmites which further enhance the mysterious mood.   There is also a nativity scene below the water which magically appears and then drifts again from view.

DESTINATION II   ALBEROBELLO   Dei Trulli Hotel

When it is time to leave Ravello, there is an efficient expressway south to the "toe" of Italy.   But for those who are enroute to Brindisi or who have the luxury of time for another adventure, I am going to include a deviation to the eastern coast, to the wonderous town of ALBEROBELLO.

I suggest an early start as there are several sightseeing stops recommended enroute.   First of all, I definitely would make the short side trip south to visit the spectacular ancient Greek city of PAESTUM.   Magically, as soon as you enter the gates of the ancient city you enter a peaceful environment of a lovely country meadow whose grass is dotted with some of the world's best preserved Greek temples.   As you walk the remains of the streets criss-crossing the city, your senses are enhanced by birds singing and the scent of roses.   It is a delightful experience.   (Before leaving Paestum you might want to stop for a snack at a lovely restaurant, MARINI SEA GARDEN, which is in a garden whose gates open onto the west side of the excavation. The Marini Sea Garden restaurant is an old villa with an attractive dining room plus a garden terrace cafe.) To reach Paestum take the Amalfi coastal road from Ravello to Salerno and then join the expressway for about 12 miles until the turnoff for Paestum which is located on a side road about a half hour drive from the freeway.

When you rejoin the expressway continue east for about 14 miles until the high-way splits. At this point take the left branch heading east toward Potenza. About 70 miles beyond the branch of the highway, watch for the exit leading to the town of MATERA. Located about a half an hour's drive north of the expressway, Matera is a strange, spooky, ghost town with a weird setting amongst ravines and deep gorges. The old town of Matera clings to the side of a hill crowned by a modern city. To visit the the lower "lost city" whose crumbling buildings melt into the rocks is a fascinating experience.

From Matera continue on the road leading northeast to ALBEROBELLO. Here are some of the strangest structures in Italy - the TRULLI. These are circu-lar stone buildings usually built in small clusters standing crisply white with conical slate roofs and whimsical twisted chimneys. Outside ladders frequently lead to upper stories. Often several of these houses are joined together to form a larger complex. The houses are intertwined by cobbled streets. What a strange and fascinating sight! These comical little houses form a jumble of a small village which looks like it should be inhabited by elves instead of "real" people.

Southern Italy & Sicily   87

For a hotel choice, you should certainly choose the DEI TRULLI. This hotel is located right on the outskirts of the Trulli village and is built within the ancient houses. The hotel is a cluster of some of the round little houses which are made into cottages scattered within a large park-like setting. Pine trees line the small paths which join the cluster of hotel rooms. Each bungalow has a living room with fireplace, one or more bedrooms, a bathroom, and small patio. One of the Trulli houses has been made into a dining room and another into the office. There is also a swimming pool and a tiny park with play equipment for the children.

Hotel Dei Trulli
Alberobello

The Trulli houses are not confined to the town of Alberobello although this is where you will find them composing an entire village. In fact, the Trulli houses you will see in the vicinity of Alberobello are sometimes more interesting than those in the town itself. As you drive along the small roads you will spot gorgeous villas cleverly converted from Trulli houses that are now obviously the homes of wealthy Italians. Other Trulli cottages are now farm houses with goats munching their lunch in the front yard. Occasionally you will spot a charming old Trulli home cozily nestled in the center of a vineyard. But most fun of all are the Trulli homes of the free spirits! Their homes, instead of the typical white exteriors, have been painted a brilliant yellow or pink or bright green with contrasting shutters.

As you are exploring the countryside around Alberobello you might want to take the short drive north to see the CASTELLANA CAVES where in a two hour tour you will see many rooms of richly colored stalagmites and stalagtites.

DESTINATION III   TROPEA   Baia Paraelios

Note: Alberobello is only about forty-five miles from BRINDISI. Brindisi is the popular port from which to take the ferry to Corfu and on to Greece. Alberobello is only about thirty-five miles from BARI which is the port to use for ferries to Dubrovnik. So, if your plans are to continue your travel adventures by boat, then Alberobello is most strategically positioned. In both Bari and Brindisi you can turn in your rental car if your holiday in Italy has ended.

However, for the rest of "our tour" the itinerary continues on to the exciting destination of Sicily. When you leave Alberobello take the road south to the coast. You might want to make a stop to see the ancient port of TARANTO which is connected by a bridge to the modern city of Taranto. Even if you are not interested in ancient history you might enjoy seeing the Italian naval ships - giant grey monsters sitting in the protected harbor.

From Taranto continue along the arch of Italy's boot until you come to Sibari where there is a short road leading east to join the main Expressway. When you are again on the Highway A3 continue south for only a few miles until you come to the exit for the tiny spur which juts up from the toe of Italy's boot and continue along the coast toward the town of TROPEA, located near the point of the peninsula.

Baia Paraelios
Tropea-Paraghelia

Just before Tropea, a sign on the right of the road points to the HOTEL BAIA PARAELIOS, a very special hotel creating a wonderful combination of a beach holiday with your sightseeing. The hotel is a cluster of cottages, cleverly spaced at various levels leading down to the beach. Each cottage has a sitting room and one or more bedrooms plus a private terrace. Although not old, a definite "inn" feeling prevails. The small reception room at the crest of the slope has lovely prints on the wall, baskets of flowers, a few antiques, and the definite flavor of good taste. The cottages are quite appealing with tiled floors and earth tone colors. There is a swimming pool on one of the "mid" levels plus at beach edge nice lounges and a delightful dining room with an outdoor terrace for summer meals. However, I saved the best for last. Stretching in front of the hotel is the most beautiful creamy-white sand beach that I saw in Italy!

Just a few miles beyond the hotel (which is officially located in the town of Paraghelia - which is so small it never shows up on any maps) is the town of TROPEA. An ancient fishing village, Tropea is perched on cliffs overhanging the beautiful blue sea. The town is most colorful and definitely worth a visit!

DESTINATION IV   TAORMINA   Hotel Timeo

When it is time to leave the Baia Paraelios, return to the expressway and continue south the short distance to the tip of the toe and take the exit to Villa San Giovanni. The route to the ferry is clearly marked. The boat ferries leave at least twice an hour for the thirty minute trip to Sicily. After buying your ticket you drive your car to the indicated lane and wait with all the trucks and campers and other cars for the signal to drive onto the boat. When on board you can leave your car and go upstairs to a lounge area where snacks can be purchased while traversing the short channel.

When the ferry arrives in MESSINA follow the freeway signals to TAORMINA, about a half an hour's drive south. Once in town follow the signs to the center of the village and with a little bit of luck you will see the sign for the HOTEL TIMEO, located at the end of a little lane just by the main entrance to the ancient city. There is sometimes a barrier at the street leading to the hotel because it is closed to all but guests of the hotel. However, just move the barrier and drive to the end of the lane and you will see the hotel.

The Hotel Timeo is a delightful hotel. If you enjoy wonderful villas your heart will be won immediately as you enter the front garden festooned with a canopy of brilliant bougenvillias and pots of brightly colored geraniums. There is a charming dining room, but best of all is the terrace where meals can be enjoyed with a bewitching vista of the gorgeous blue bay - behind which majestically towers Mount Etna.   A path immediately behind the hotel leads up to the major sightseeing destination in Taormina, the enormous Greek Theater.   I would splurge and ask for a room with a view balcony.   There could not be many places in the world with a gift of such an incredibly splendid panorama.   The Hotel Timeo has been in the same family for over a hundred years and this continuity of loving ownership is apparent in every delightful detail from the fresh flowers on the tables to the excellent and beautifully served meals.

Hotel Timeo
Sicily, Taormina

The town of Taormina is also delightful.   As if glued to the top of a small penin-sula, Taormina juts out to the sea and then drops steeply to the coast below. Quaint, colorful streets wind through the village where you can browse in the gift shops, visit small churches, enjoy a cappucino at a little cafe, or simply enjoy the view.

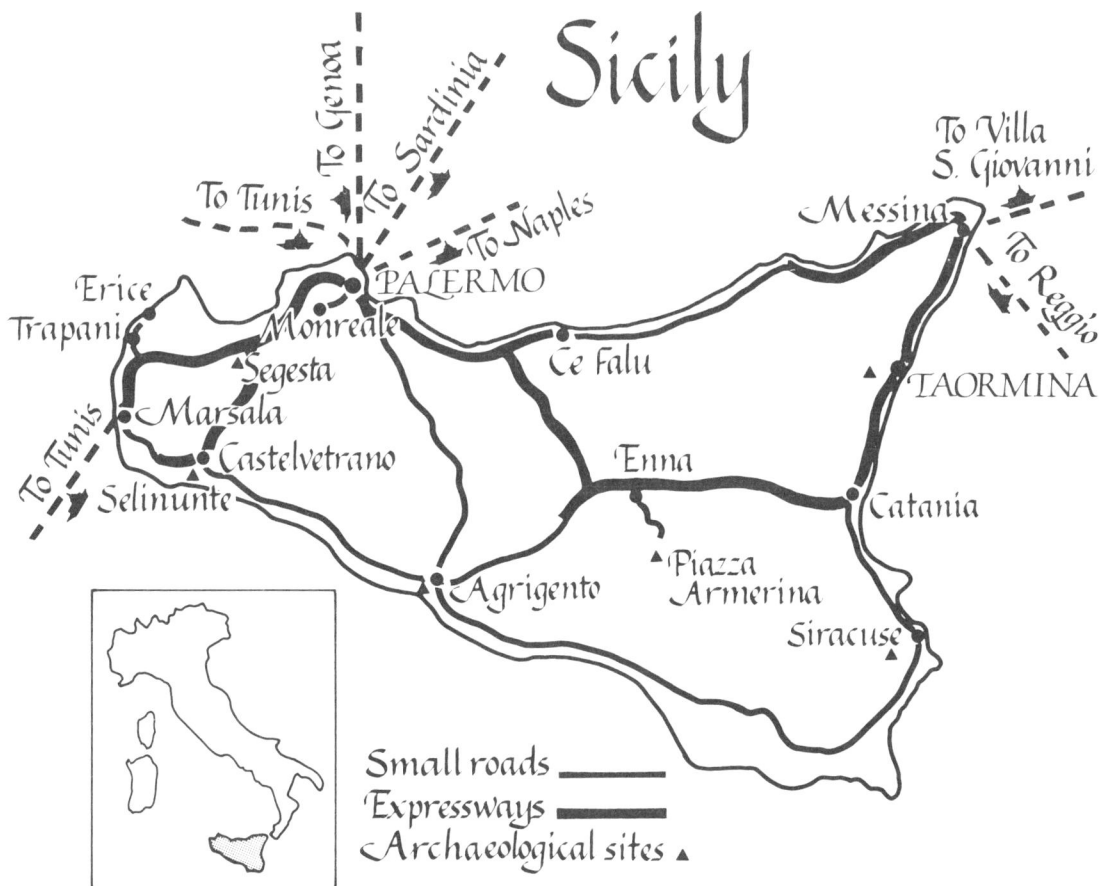

Sicily

Map labels:
- To Genoa
- To Sardinia
- To Tunis
- To Naples
- PALERMO
- Erice
- Trapani
- Monreale
- Segesta
- To Tunis
- Marsala
- Castelvetrano
- Selinunte
- Ce Falu
- Enna
- Agrigento
- Piazza Armerina
- Siracuse
- Catania
- TAORMINA
- Messina
- To Villa S. Giovanni
- To Reggio

Legend:
Small roads ——
Expressways ▬▬
Archaeological sites ▲

From Taormina follow the freeway south toward CATANIA. Be forewarned that the freeway bypassing the city is not yet finished and until it is you will have to follow a maze of streets as signs lead you through the congested traffic. Have hope though.   Finally you will emerge at the outskirts of the city where the freeway continues on to PALERMO.   Before heading for Palermo you might want to take the approximately 80 mile round trip excursion south to SYRACUSE which is an ancient Greek city dating back seven hundred years before Christ.   The Greeks loved beauty and here overlooking a gorgeous blue bay they built their theatres, temples, and coliseums .   Of special interest is an enormous theatre over four hundred feet across.

Enna is about an hours drive west from Catania.   Should you want to include another short deviation, about twenty miles south of Enna is the town of PIAZZA ARMERINA.   About four miles southwest of town there are some excellent mosaics in the remains of an ancient Roman villa - the VILLA OF CASALE. Returning to Enna take the expressway north toward the coast and then head west to PALERMO.

Palermo is a large city with lots of traffic and new construction.   However it makes a good base from which to explore some of the jewels of Sicily and luckily there is a splendid hotel here, the GRAND HOTEL VILLA IGIEA.   Actually the hotel is much more like a small castle than a villa.   It is an oasis in a bustling city.   The hotel is located on the ocean right next to the harbor.   The entrance is rather formal and grand.   The bedrooms are large and nicely furnished in a traditional motif and those in the rear have a lovely view over the back garden to the sea.   There is a pool in the garden which even sports its own miniature Greek temple.

Grand Hotel Villa Igiea
Sicily, Palermo

From Palermo are many fascinating excursions. A circle trip from Palermo includes some of Sicily's finest archaeological sites. To begin your journey take the expressway west toward TRAPANI. About five miles after the highway splits you will see a sign for SEGESTA which is located only a few minutes from the expressway. Here in a remote mountain area stands a delightful Greek Doric temple - practically perfect in its preservation. In fact, many experts consider this to be one of the finest Greek Doric temples in the world today. But one of the most superb aspects of this temple is its location. There is nothing to jar the senses. Reached by a path leading up from the parking area the temple is located on a small hill. All around is great natural beauty. After visiting the temple return to the parking area and follow the signs up the hill for another treat - a small, but beautiful Greek theatre. Again, the location is what makes this theatre so special. What an eye the Greeks had for beauty! The stage is set in such a way that the spectators look out across the mountains to the sea.

Just north of Trapani is the ancient town of ERICE perched on rocks soaring over 2,000 feet in the clouds. This is a fascinating walled city filled with colorful medieval houses.

South of Trapani the road circles the island and passes through MARSALA which gives its name to the famous Marsala wine of the region.

The next destination is the great Greek ruins at SELINUNTE. As you near Castelvetrano watch for signs for the coastal archaeological site. Here by the ocean are the impressive remains of some of the most gigantic temples left by the Greeks. It is staggering to imagine how the Greeks more than twenty-five hundred years ago could have pieced together the huge blocks of rock weighing over one hundred tons each! From Selinunte the expressway heads directly north for your return to Palermo.

Another recommended side trip from Palermo would be to visit the ancient fishing village of CEFALU built on a rocky peninsula about an hour's drive east from Palermo. Not only is this a very colorful fishing village complete with brightly hued boats and twisting narrow streets, but there is also a splendid Norman cathedral. It was built by King Roger in the 12th century in fulfillment of a promise to God for sparing his life during a storm at sea.

Two of Palermo's major sights are luckily only a few miles from the city. In MONREALE located about five miles south of Palermo is an awesome Cathedral which is especially famous for its beautiful mosaic panels showing a strong Moorish influence. Reading from left to right these one hundred thirty pictures depict the complete cycle of both the Old and the New Testaments. The bronze doors of the Cathedral are also beautiful and were done by Bonanno Pisano, a famous 12th century artist. The other sight close to Palermo is MONTE PELLEGRINO, just west of the city. Here is a cave which has been transformed into a chapel commemorating Santa Rosalia, a Duke's daughter who became a hermit - living and dying in this cave.

There is still another very important archaeological site on Sicily - the ruins of of the VALLEY OF THE TEMPLES at ARGRIGENTO.   There is no doubt that this ancient Greek city, with the Temple of Juno, the Temple of Concord, the Temple of Hercules, the Temple of Jupiter, and the Temple of the Dioscuri is a marvelous example of the tremendous wealth, power, and skills of the ancient Greeks.   Because this excursion takes such a long drive of which only a short portion is freeway and because there is no excellent inn to recommend for the night, it seems that the wealth of temples that are more easily accessible will probably suffice for all but the most ardent ancient Greek enthusiast. When it is time to leave Sicily Palermo is a convenient gateway.   From here you can fly back to Rome making a connection to your homeward flight or else you can take a ferry back to Naples, Genoa, Sardinia, or even Tunis.

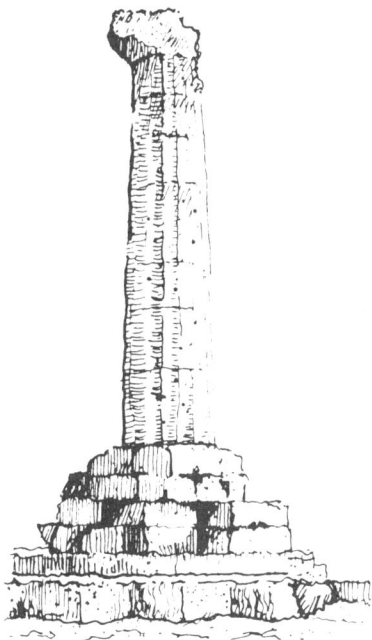

Southern Italy & Sicily

INDEX of HOTELS REFERENCED by MAP NUMBER

Italy

SWITZERLAND

AUSTRIA

FRANCE

Milan

Genoa

YUGOSLAVIA

Venice

Adriatic Sea

Ligurian Sea

Florence

CORSICA

Tyrrhenian Sea

Rome

Naples

Brindisi

SARDINIA

Mediterranean Sea

SICILY

Ionian Sea

There is a fascinating section in south eastern Italy where there is a collection of strange round white buildings with grey stone conical shaped roofs.   These ancient houses seem to be "left over" from some Moorish tribe which most have inhabited this part of Italy long ago.   These houses are called "Trulli" and usually are seen in groups of two or three.   In the town of Alberobello there is actually a whole village of the comical little houses whose jumble of domed roofs, whitewashed walls, and crooked little chimneys create a most unusual sight!   Fortunately there is a superb hotel in the area that is located within walking distance of the Trulli village.   Not only is its location excellent, but the hotel captures the mood of the area since it is constructed within some of the ancient trulli houses.   Small bungalows are scattered around a large park like area connected by winding pathways under the pine trees.   Each bungalow is actually a suite with a modern bathroom, a living room with fireplace, one or more bedrooms, and a private patio.   The dining rooms and the reception area each occupy their own "trulli".   Within the grounds a pool and children's play yard have been added.   If you are on your way to Greece or Yugoslavia you will find the Hotel Dei Trulli an excellent choice since it is very close to Brindisi and Bari, the two major ferry ports.

HOTEL DEI TRULLI
Manager: Luigi Farace
Via Cadore
70011 Alberobello, Italy
tel: (080) 721 130 telex 810311
34 rooms - moderate
Near the "heel" of Italy
Swimming pool - small park

Hotel Descriptions

The Villa Cipriani is just as I had envisioned in every dream of Italy: an old villa snuggled on a hill; her softly faded exterior emphasized by dark green shutters; masses of roses creeping over trellises; columns adorned with vines; lazy views over rolling green hills; faded ochre-colored walls half hidden by tall Cypress trees dotting nearby hilltops; birds singing in the garden; the sentimental rhythmical peal of church bells; a pianist on the terrace playing old love songs; the fragrance of flowers drifting through the air like the finest perfume; a balmy night under the stars - perfection!   My impression of a romantic paradise must not have been a unique experience for in the garden was a wedding party. A beautiful bride - a handsome groom; they had fallen in love at the Cipriani and had returned with family and friends from the United States for their marriage!

The Villa Cipriani is located in Asolo, a charming, small, medieval, walled, hill town less than two hours north of Venice. It has an atmosphere so delightful that Robert Browning chose it as a residence.   And the home he chose?   The Cipriani.   Luckily, the home is now a hotel and you, too, can "live" in Asolo.

HOTEL VILLA CIPRIANI
Manager: Giuseppe Kamenar
Via Canova, 298
31011 Asolo, Italy
tel: (0423) 55 444, telex 411060
32 rooms - expensive
Credit cards: all major

Beautiful Old Villa
About 40 miles NW of Venice

One of the joys of researching a guidebook is to discover a "jewel" of an inn.   It is rather like a treasure hunt.   Rarely though do we find an excellent hotel which we have not heard of previously.   However, The Country House is just such a find.   It is located on a small lane less than half a mile from the lower gates into Assisi.   The inn is actually an ancient peasant's cottage which Silvana Ciammarvghi, the owner, has lovingly restored and transformed into a small pension.   It is not surprising that the hotel is so loaded with charm, for Silvana loves antiques and has an eye for beautiful wooden chests, tables, chairs, mirrors, and beds.   In fact, the first floor of this inn is an antique shop.   Most of the furniture in the house is for sale but, no problem; when a piece is sold, another takes its place from the shop downstairs!   All of the rooms have style and taste and are decorated with an antique "country" ambiance.

The "Country House" has only recently opened and Silvana Ciammarvghi, who is charming and speaks excellent English, will be glad to welcome you to her "home" which would make an excellent location for exploring Umbria.

ANTICHITA "THREE ESSE" COUNTRY HOUSE
Proprietor: Silvana Ciammarvghi
S. Pietro
06081 Assisi, Italy
Phone: (075) 816 363
12 rooms - inexpensive - budget
Breakfast only served
Inn combined with antique shop
Countryside location near Assisi
About 110 miles north of Rome

The Hotel Subasio is located with one wall forming part of the ancient square in front of the Basilica of St. Francis.   In fact, the hotel is actually linked to the Basilica by an arched colonnade.   The setting is marvelous with the rear of the hotel facing the beautiful Umbrian countryside.   On the lower level there are several delightful view terraces romantically shaded by vines.   Many of the rooms also have splendid views over the Umbrian valley.   Request one of the deluxe rooms with a view balcony.   These are marvelous.

The public rooms of the Subasio are pleasant, but rather stilted and formal. However, you will not be inside much anyway.   The terraces are magic!   To sit and watch the lovely fields mellow in the evening sun with that very special glow which is so characteristic of Umbria is certainly one of life's real pleasures! It is no wonder that many celebrities have chosen the Hotel Subasio for residence when visiting Assisi; such famous names as Charlie Chaplin and James Stewart grace the guest book. It deserves its wonderful reputation. Andrea Rossi personally oversees the management of the hotel and there is a friendliness in the air from the gentle maid who turns down your bed in the evening right to the charming waiter who helps select your local wine with dinner.

HOTEL SUBASIO
Owner: Andrea E. Rossi
Via Frate Ella, 2
06081 Assisi, Italy
tel:(075) 812 206 telex: 662029
70 rooms – moderate
Credit cards: all major
About 110 miles north of Rome

For a splendid, moderately priced little inn just off the Piazza del Comune in the heart of Assisi, the Hotel Umbra is a wonderful choice.   If you are expecting a luxury hotel with fancy decor, this will not be the hotel for you.   Although the public rooms have accents of antiques and a cozy ambiance, they are "homey" rather than grand.   The bedrooms, which are clean and fresh, are simple rather than deluxe.   Nevertheless, because of the absolutely delightful small terrace at the entrance which is oozing with charm, the Umbra would have won my heart even if the inside had been a disaster.   You reach the Umbra by way of a narrow little alley leading off from the Piazza del Commune.   The entrance is through wrought iron gates which open to a tiny patio - a green oasis of peace and quiet where tables are set under a trellis covered with vines whose leaves provide shade and paint a lacey pattern of shadows.   From this intimate terrace there is a lovely view.   Some of the bedrooms, too, have a panoramic vista of the Umbrian hills and valley.   There is a cute little dining room and several small drawing rooms.   This small, family owned and managed hotel is a real asset to the wonderful medieval city of Assisi.

HOTEL UMBRA
Owner: Family Alberto Laudenzi
Via degli Archi
06081 Assisi, Italy
tel: (075) 812 240   telex: 66122
27 rooms - inexpensive
Credit cards: all major
Central location off main square
Open December through October
About 110 miles north of Rome

The Hotel Castello di Balsorano is a castle lover's dream.
everything a castle should have!   Like any proper castle it sit:
its own little mountain.   You wind up the hill then pass through the outer g
and into a forest.   Next you pass through a tunnel-like entrance and into the
courtyard.   The reception area is to your right and opens onto a wonderful
medieval style dining room.   Everything is authentic from the coats of armor,
battle banners, shields and daggers to the antique beds.   In fact, the hotel is
open to the public who come just to tour this great old masterpiece.   It is the
lucky few who are able to spend the night!

The hotel bedrooms have some wonderful old furniture and lots of character, but
they are a bit shabby.   However, as you wander through the castle you can
certainly appreciate what a tremendous undertaking it would be to keep this
enormous castle in perfect condition.   And the price is right.   This is a very
reasonable hotel and if it were in mint condition would be a luxury rather than
budget establishment.   There is another real PLUS.   The owner's wife, Mary
Ricci, is English, and her gracious hospitality will make your castle interlude
even more special.

Hotel Castello di Balsorano
Mary & Nino Ricci
67025 Balsorano, Italy
tel: (0863) 95236
6 rooms - inexpensive - budget
Closed November
Atmospheric old hilltop castle
Located about 80 miles E. Rome

For a moderately priced hotel in the charming ancient port of Bellagio, the Hotel Florence just can't be surpassed.   The location is prime; right on the main square with even its own little tea terrace shaded by trees across the street by the lake where you can have a snack while watching the boat traffic.   If you are lucky enough to snare a front room with a balcony, you can step out through your French doors and be treated to a splendid view of Lake Como.

There is a small reception area and then, down a few steps, there is an intimate lounge with a fireplace, beamed ceilings, and some chairs set around tiny tables.   A staircase leads upstairs to simple but adequate bedrooms and to a guest dining room which has a fireplace and wooden ladderback chairs.

The hotel is owned by the Ketzlar family, who are real pros; the inn has been in their family for a hundred and fifty years.   I met Mrs. Freidl Ketzlar and her daughter, Roberta.   They both speak excellent English and are extremely warm and gracious.

HOTEL FLORENCE
Proprietors: Ketzlar Family
22021 Bellagio (Lake Como)
Italy
tel: (031) 950 342
48 rooms - inexpensive
Open April 25 - Oct 10
Credit cards: all major
Village center, near ferry
About 48 miles north Milan

The Grand Hotel Villa Serbelloni is certainly appropriately named. It definitely is GRAND!   In fact, the public rooms are almost overwhelming with intricately painted ceilings, gold mirrors, fancy columns, Oriental rugs, gilded chairs, heavy chandeliers, and a sweeping marble staircase. The bedrooms are quite nice, although I did not think the decor too outstanding.   However, the quality is superb: lovely percale sheets, soft down pillows, and large towels. The service, too, is excellent.

Located in the gardens by the lake there is a large swimming pool.   If you prefer sightseeing or shopping to swimming, the colorful old port of Bellagio is just steps from the hotel.   If you tire of exploring the town of Bellagio, the ferry is only a few minutes from the hotel.   Or, if you want to be discreet, the concierge can arrange a special boat to pick you up at the private pier in front of the hotel.

Perhaps the original grandeur of the Grand Hotel Villa Serbelloni has faded a little, but if ornate elegance and the feeling of living in a masterpiece of a palace appeals to you, I think you will enjoy your stay here.   Pretend you are a guest at a weekend house party - given by Royalty, of course!

GRAND HOTEL VILLA SERBELLONI
Proprietor: Rudy Bucher
22021 Bellagio, Italy
tel: (031) 950 216   telex:380330
100 rooms - very expensive
Credit cards: AX VS
Sumptuous palace on Lake Como
About 48 miles north of Milan

How lucky to find a "picture perfect" inn in the splendid ancient upper town of Bergamo (Citta Alta).   And what a picture!   The Hotel Agnello d'Oro sits just off the main piazza Viejo, smugly facing its own tiny, intimate square, complete with tinkling fountain.   The hotel is tall and skinny - only two rooms wide but rising six stories high!   Inside, too, this old hotel is great.   An ancient desk is in the tiny lobby and to the right is a wonderful restaurant with crowds of copper, plenty of colorful old plates on the walls, cozy chairs and wooden tables covered with bright red and white checked table cloths.   The effect is cluttered but, oh, so gay!   Upstairs the rooms are not for the fussy.   They are very basic, but they are perfect for those on a budget whose love of romantic ambiance surpasses their desire for perfection in sleeping quarters.   Even the fussy among you might adore waking up in the morning, opening the French doors, and stepping out onto your tiny balcony to greet the day.   The front rooms are prime, with flower boxes on the iron railings.   An area of potted row-hedge defines the outdoor terrace.   The building is an olive drab with brown shutters and has an awning in front.   Another plus - although the government gives the Hotel Agnello D'Oro a third class rating, Michelin gives a two fork approval to the restaurant!

AGNELLO D'ORO
Via Gombito 22
24100 Bergamo (Citta Alta)
Italy
tel: (035) 249 883
25 rooms - inexpensive - budget
Marvelous walled medieval city
Located about 30 miles NE Milan

In 1550, King John of Portugal decided to give a little gift to the Emperor Ferdinand of Austria, so he purchased an elephant in India, shipped it to Genoa, then planned to "walk" it to Austria.   This giant beast grew weary about the time it reached Bressanone and was stabled for two weeks at the "Am Hohen Feld" Inn. Young and old came from miles around to see this impromptu "circus." The proprietor of the Am Hohen Feld was obviously a master at marketing.   To maintain the fame of his establishment, he promptly renamed his hotel - you guessed it - The "Elefant".   A picture of our friend the elephant was painted on the front of the building commemorating the sensational event. But even without an elephant story this hotel is a winner.   Although the bedrooms themselves are a little drab, they are immaculately clean and comfortable.   In contrast to the simplicity of the bedrooms, the reception areas and dining rooms are fantastic, incorporating beautiful antiques, museum quality paintings, magnificent paneling, all of which are combined with great taste.   But, even if there were no elephant story nor an antique ambiance to the hotel, the Elefant has another tremendous attribute; the food is fantastic! Most of the eggs, butter, milk, fruit, and vegetables, and even the wine, come from the hotel's own farms.

HOTEL ELEFANT
Proprietor: Wolfgang Heiss
Via Rio Bianco, 4
I-39042 Bressanone, Italy
tel: (0472) 22 288
45 rooms - moderate
Open March to Nov 12 - Pool
NE Italy near Brenner Pass

The Cenobio dei Dogi was formerly the summer home of the Genoese Doges, so it is no wonder that it has such an idyllic location nestled on a small hill which forms one end of Camogli's miniature half-moon bay.　From the hotel terrace there is an enchanting view of the tiny cove lined with marvelous narrow old fishermen's cottages painted in all shades of ochres and siennas.　The hotel has a very nice swimming pool, plus a private (though pebbly) beach.　Many of the bedrooms have balconies which boast romantic views of this storybook scene. For tennis buffs, there is a tennis court, although I cannot imagine anyone wanting to play tennis with all the beautiful walking trails which make enticing spider web designs on the peninsula.

Although the Cenobio Dei Dogi is larger than most hotels which appear in this guide and decor does not radiate antique ambiance, it possesses a solid, comfortable, no-nonsense kind of charm.　It is not chic in the "Jet Set" style of hotels frequently found on the Riviera, but if you relate to gorgeous flower gardens, exceptional views, and slightly faded, "old world" comfort in one of the most picturesque villages in Italy, then I think you will love this hotel.

HOTEL CENOBIO DEI DOGI
Via Niccolo Cuneo, 34
16032 Camogli, Italy
tel: (0185) 770041 telex: 211116
84 rooms - expensive
Closed January and February
Former summer Doges' palace
Pool, private beach, tennis
Near Portofino - Italian Riviera

The Grand Hotel Quisiana conjures up the image of a Hollywood setting where the jet-set gather.   The women, adorned in jewels and the latest swimming ensembles, sit in the sun and gossip about the latest scandal while their husbands (or boyfriends?) sit pool-side drinking scotch and playing the game of grown boys - discussing their latest business ventures.   But it is all great fun and quite in the mood of Capri which has been a playground for the wealthy since the time of the early Romans.

The Grand Hotel Quisiana is a deluxe hotel with a gorgeous oval pool overlooking the blue Mediterranean.   The air of formal elegance appears as soon as you enter the lobby decorated with marble floors, soft green velvet chairs, Oriental carpets, ornate statues, crystal chandelier and beautiful paintings. All the bedrooms are well appointed and the deluxe rooms even have separate "his" and "hers" half-baths.   Room rates include breakfast and lunch or dinner and you can choose from almost anything on the menu.   The Grand Hotel Quisiana most definitely provides a setting and atmosphere to reflect the image of, and cater to their jet-set clientele.

GRAND HOTEL QUISIANA
Manager: G. Chervatin
Via Camerelle 2
80073 Capri, Italy
tel:(081) 8370 788 telex:710520
143 rooms - very expensive
Credit cards: all major

Beautiful pool in garden setting

The Hotel Luna savors one of the most beautiful locations on the Island of Capri. It is just a short walk from the main town yet, in atmosphere, it seems miles away from the bustle and noise.   The hotel is perched on the cliffs overlooking the spectacular coastline of green hills that drop straight into the sea and from which emerge giant rock formations.   There is an outside terrace for dining which captures this view, plus the premium rooms have balconies overlooking the sea.   There is a very large pool which is surrounded by flowers.   The pool is located a short stroll from the hotel and also has a splendid view.

The decor of the hotel seems to be in need of refreshing.   The overstuffed chairs and velvets and heavy furniture seem to conflict with the natural splendor of the landscape. However, the natural attributes are such that I think the hotel is definitely one of the best on Capri.   The overall mood at the hotel is set by its delightful entrance.   There is a covered trellis walkway which, in summer, is completely shaded by brilliant bougainvillea and grape vines and bordered by flowers. It is a wonderful introduction to the Hotel Luna and to what I am sure would make a lovely interlude by the sea.

HOTEL LUNA
Via Matteotti, 3
80073 Capri, Italy
tel: (081) 8370433 telex: 721247
Open April to October
48 rooms - expensive
Credit cards: all major
On cliff above the sea
Lovely views & lovely pool

The Gaidello Club is unique in this guide series.   This is the first time that an inn has been included which cannot be booked on an individual basis.   I did not know this when I first wrote to Paola Giovanna Bini and, after stopping for lunch - with the best pasta I have EVER tasted - it was too late; my heart was won!   It was easy to rationalize that frequently families or friends travel together and so a "group" of eight (which is the minimum number that Paola will accept in her inn) is not an impossibility; hence, The Villa Gaidello is here in print.

The Gaidello Club has been for many generations the country home of the Bini family.   Ten years ago, Paola Giovanna Bini assumed the awesome task of reconstructing the two hundred and fifty year old farm house into a working operation.   Part of the farm now provides four apartments, each apartment with one private bath.   The apartments are very simple.   However, what is truly special about this inn is the food, which is absolutely marvelous.   Only the freshest vegetables and fruits are served.   All the pasta is prepared the same day.   The wines come from their own vineyard.   Even the liqueur served after the meal is made from walnuts in the orchard.   Nothing could be more delicious!

GAIDELLO CLUB
Proprietor: Paola Giovanna Bini
Via Gaidello, 22
Castelfranco Emilia, Italy
tel: (059) 926 806
4 suites - moderate
Only groups of 8 to 13 persons
Cooking classes can be arranged
About 18 miles west of Bologna

The Tenuta di Ricavo is unique. It is not a "hotel" at all in the usual connotation, but rather a tiny village with peasant's cottages which have been transformed into delightful little guest rooms. The stables are now the dining room and the barn is now the office. You enter the parklike setting through a huge pine forest where small cottages are nestled in amongst the trees. Gardens are everywhere and roses embellish the weathered stone cottages giving them a fairy-tale appearance. The total effect is absolutely enchanting!

Originally the town was the summer residence of a Swiss family who used it for holidays and later transformed their village into an exquisite resort. The family seeks no publicity. They do not need it. The hotel is always filled with fortunate guests who have discovered this paradise. However, this inn definitely is not for everyone. It is quiet. It is remote. It is unstructured. But, it is a haven for the traveler for whom a good book, a walk through the forest, a swim in the pool, a drink at sunset with fellow guests, and a delicious dinner are fulfillment.

TENUTA DI RICAVO
Family Lobrano-Scotoni
53011 Castellina in Chianti
Italy
tel: (577) 740 221
25 rooms - moderate
Unique village hotel -3 day minimum
Pool and 300 acre park
Hotel is comprised of small village
Tuscany Hills - south of Florence

The Villa Casalecchi is a beautiful Italian villa, turned into a small hotel, which still manages to retain the warmth and graciousness of the private home that it once was.   The Villa Casalecchi has been in the same family for many years, and when I arrived, the daughter, who grew up in the villa, showed me around.

You enter the lovely parklike estate via a winding road which weaves through a serene pine forest.   The woods set the romantic mood for this old villa which is cleverly built to capture the views of the Tuscany hills.   The lobby, lounges, and dining rooms are very comfortable and contain many of the family antiques. There are only fifteen guest rooms which vary in decor as they would if you were a guest in a private home.   On a terrace behind the villa is a swimming pool which is on a lower level from the hotel and overlooks the rolling hillside.

The Villa Casalecchi is host every year to a small group of artists from the United States.   Mrs. Casalecchi told me that the students depart each day in a different direction, paints in hand, to capture the gorgeous Tuscany landscapes. I can't imagine a more delightful artistic holiday!

VILLA CASALECCHI
Family Casalecchi
53011 Castellina in Chianti
Italy
tel: (577) 740 240
15 rooms - moderate
Credit cards: all major
Pool and parklike setting
Tuscany Hills - south of Florence

A book on the most charming hotels in Italy could not be complete without including one of the queens of the world, the Villa D'Este.   Originally the hotel was a private villa built in 1568 by the Cardinal Tolomeo Gallio.   He obviously had elegant (and expensive) taste, for the Villa D'Este is truly a fantasy land. From the moment you enter the enormous lobby with the sweeping staircase, marble, crystal, soaring ceilings, statues, and columns surround you. Everything is elaborate and ornate.   Upstairs, the bedrooms are all very similar in decor with color coordinated carpets, walls, and bedspreads. Some of the bedrooms have prime locations overlooking the lake.   Although the interior is beautiful it is the outside where the fun really begins.   There is a terrace immediately in front of the hotel with tables set for drinks or dining and then a dock for boats and a large pool suspended over the lake.   Tennis?   Of course. Horse back riding?   Nearby.   Golf?   Can be arranged.   However, the most stunning feature of the Villa D'Este is the park which surrounds it with lovely pathways winding between trees, a jogging course, glorious flowers, statues, and even a formal garden with a dramatic mosaic colonnade.

VILLA D'ESTE
Manager: Mario Arrigo
22010 Cernobbio, Italy
tel: (31) 511471   telex: 380025
180 rooms - very expensive
Open April - October

Credit cards: all major
Pool and tennis
Located on the W shore Lake Como

The Anna Maria is located in Champoluc which is a small town almost at the end of the beautiful Ayas Valley which stretches north into the Alps almost to the Swiss border in northwest Italy.   As you drive through the town of Champoluc you will see a small sign for the Anna Maria on the right side of the road just before you leave town.   Turn right on this little lane which winds up the hill and you will see the Anna Maria on your right set in a serene pine grove.   The Anna Maria is not a luxury hotel, but rather an old mountain chalet which is now a simple, but very charming inn.   There is a large deck for sunning which stretches across the entrance.   Inside there is a cozy dining room - my favorite room - which exudes warmth and coziness with its wooden alpine style country chairs, wooden tables, and gay red checked curtains at the windows.   Upstairs the bedrooms are not luxurious, but most inviting with wooden paneling on the walls and a rustic ambiance, and best of all - every bedroom has a private bathroom.   Perhaps the most winning feature is Anna Maria, the owner, who is your hostess and oversees her little inn with a gracious charm.   The atmosphere is one of "homey" ambiance - not for the fussy but wonderful for those who love the friendliness of a country inn in a mountain village.

ANNA MARIA
Owner: Anna Maria
11020 Champoluc, Italy
tel: (0125) 307 128
25 rooms - inexpensive
excellent value
Open July-Aug & Dec-mid Apr
Chalet style - lovely setting
Mountain location - NW Italy

The Hotel Menardi, dates back eight hundred years. Originally it was a peasant's farmhouse, but as Cortina's popularity as a fabulous ski center has spread so has the town, and now the farm is located right on the outskirts of town on the main road heading north.   Nevertheless, the Menardi family, who have owned the home for a century and a half, have managed to maintain the country flavor through the use of many antiques, marvelous old prints on the walls, old clocks, giant dowry chests, oriental carpets, beautiful hanging cupboards - and all set off by the warmth and gaiety of flowers everywhere.   The bedrooms vary in decor but are all pleasant and with private bath.   A chalet behind the hotel plus a deluxe addition that is being built will increase the number of bedrooms.

It seems that the Menardi farm just naturally evolved into a hotel.   At first it gave shelter to the men carting loads over the Cimabanche Pass who needed a place to sleep - more often than not in the hay loft!   Today the inn is a simple but wonderful small hotel whose special ingredient is the old fashioned warmth and hospitality of the gracious Menardi family.

HOTEL MENARDI
Owner: Angelo Menardi Family
112 Via Majon
32043 Cortina D'Ampezzo, Italy
tel: (436) 2400
40 rooms - inexpensive
excellent value
Open Jul-Sep, late Dec-Mar
Old farmhouse - many antiques
Located in the Dolomites -NE Italy

The Castello Di Pomerio dates from the 9th Century and has been restored with exquisite taste and quality.   As you roam the antique filled rooms, you will be aware of the impact of the perfection that is everywhere.   Each detail of restoration shows loving care.   In fact, even ancient frescoes have been meticulously restored.   Some of the bedrooms are in the main castle and others are in a wing across the road that is cleverly intertwined with the castle by a tunnel so that you will still feel a part of the main hotel.   All of the bedrooms vary in decor, but all are outstanding.   Most of the ones I saw had wonderful wooden beds and attractive heavy curtains; many had cozy fireplaces...all had charm!   For the exercise enthusiast, there is a tennis court plus both an indoor and an outdoor swimming pool.

Through the ages, this hotel has changed hands many times.   At one point, its past even included use as a silk factory!   How lucky for the tourist, though, that Lital Magni Donati now owns the hotel and has turned it into a masterpiece of romantic lure where one can stop for a few days and live like a king in his "own" castle.

HOTEL CASTELLO DI POMERIO
Owner: Lital Magni Donati
Via Como, 5
22036 Pomerio di Erba, Italy
tel: (031) 611 516   telex 380463
58 rooms - moderate
Credit cards: all major
Sauna, inside and outside pools
North of Milan near Lake Como

The Punta Est is a lovely old villa perched on a hilltop overlooking the sea. When the home was converted to a villa an annex was added to provide more bedrooms.   However, it still gives the friendly feeling of a private home.   This warmth of reception and attention to detail is the result of the management of the Podesta family who own and manage the inn.   They seem dedicated to making your stay as enjoyable as possible.   Even their German Shepherd seems to want to welcome you.   There are little terraces with lovely views snuggled at various levels among the trees.   On one of these terraces is a swimming pool. Plus there is access to the public beach of Finale Ligure which can easily be reached by walking down the path to the main highway and following the tunnel beneath the highway to the beach.

The rooms in the main villa are smaller and more old-fashioned than those in the newer annex which are more reminiscent of an American motel.   There is also a small dining room for breakfast which is especially inviting with its blue and white English bone china service.   This is just one example of a very nice touch offered by owners who really want to please.

HOTEL PUNTA EST
Proprietor: Family Podesta
17024 Finale Ligure, Italy
tel: (019) 600 611
37 rooms - moderate
May 15 - Sep 20 - 3 day minimum
Italian Riviera west of Genoa
Hilltop villa overlooking sea
Pool and access to the beach

The Grand Hotel Villa Cora is a mansion!   It was originally built during the 19th century by the Baron Oppenheim as a gift for his beautiful young bride.   Among the many romantic tales of the Villa Cora is the one about Oppenheim's wife who, so the story goes, became enamoured of one of her many admirers.   The jealous baron was so enraged that he threatened to burn the entire mansion. Luckily for you and me, he was stopped in time from this mad endeavor by his friends, and today this magnificent villa is a stunning hotel.   Although only about a five minute taxi ride from the center of Florence (or a half an hour walk), the Grand Hotel Villa Cora is eons away in atmosphere.   You feel more like you are a guest in a country estate rather than in a city hotel.   The villa is set in intricate gardens and even has a pool!

The interior of the hotel is very ornate and sumptuous.   You can almost hear the sounds of laughter and music drifting through the gardens.   And indeed the mansion has always been famous for its dramatic parties.   At one time the villa was the residence of Napoleon's wife, Empress Eugenia, whose gay entertaining was the talk of Florence.   Now this grand palace-like home can be yours for days of dreams and romance!

GRAND HOTEL VILLA CORA
Viale Machiavelli 18/20
50125 Florence, Italy
tel: (055) 229 8451 telex: 570 604
56 rooms - expensive

Sumptuous villa - park-like setting
Swimming pool in a lovely garden

For location the Hermitage absolutely cannot be surpassed - only steps from the Ponte Vechio in the heart of Florence.   This pensione is on the fifth floor of an office building reached by a private elevator to which each guest is given a key upon arrival.   When the elevator reaches the fifth floor there is a small reception area and an intimate lounge and bar.   Up another flight of stairs is the prize of the hotel, a delightful outdoor terrace complete with greenery and flowers and a fabulous view over the rooftops of Florence and the Ponte Vecchio.   There is no restaurant at the Hermitage, but snacks and drinks are served either in the lounge, or better yet, on the rooftop terrace.   Since this is a budget pensione it definitely is not for those seeking luxury.   The guest rooms are extremely simple, the lounge though cozy could use a little sprucing up, and the mattresses could be better.   However, it has the attributes of great price, perfect location, delightful outdoor terrace, and excellent management.   The hotel is owned and managed by Paoli Scarelli and his charming Swedish wife, both of whom speak English.   They oversee every detail of the operation and are responsible for the personalized service and "homey" ambiance.   So for those of you who are not "fussy" and for whom location is of prime importance, the Pensione Hermitage might be the perfect choice in Florence.

PENSIONE HERMITAGE
Owner: Paolo Scarcelli
Vicolo Marzio 1
50122 Florence, Italy
tel: (55) 287 216
16 rooms - moderate - good value
Rooftop terrace with lovely view
Located in the heart of Florence

The Lungarno Hotel is superbly located directly on the Arno River and only a few minutes walk from the Ponte Vecchio.   Although most of the hotel is of new construction, the architect cleverly incorporated an ancient stone tower into the hotel so it is easy to rationalize including this hotel - one of my favorites in Florence - into this travel guide.   The interior of the hotel is traditional rather than antique in decor, but the decorating is done with excellent taste and the effect is most pleasing.   Lovely soft colors are used throughout with beautiful prints and many fresh flowers.   The bedrooms are very comfortable and those who book well in advance can request one of the rooms overlooking the Arno. Those who really plan ahead might be lucky enough to even secure one of the few rooms with a balcony overlooking the river.   What a treat to sit on your own little balcony in the evening and watch the Arno fade into gold and the Ponte Vecchio glow in the setting sun.   There are several rooms in the tower itself. One of these is especially romantic with its remaining old stone wall and its staircase that leads up to a little balcony and a third bed.   Several of the other rooms in the new portion of the hotel also have balconies which can be used as sleeping alcoves.

LUNGARNO HOTEL
Borgo San Jacopo 14
50125 Florence, Italy
tel: (055) 264 211 telex: 570129
71 rooms - moderate
Short walk to Ponte Vecchio
Wonderful location on the Arno
Some rooms with view balconies
Located in heart of Florence

Once in a while a hotel stands out like a beacon amongst its competition.   The Monna Lisa, located about a five minute walk from the heart of Florence, is just such a hotel.   Although rated as a first class pensione by the Italian government, it is a gem of a tiny hotel by anyone's standards.   The entrance is non-descript but, the drab street and exterior hide a small inn blooming with charm.   The present owner is a descendant of Giovanni Dupre, the famous sculptor, which perhaps accounts for some of the exquisite art treasures in the Monna Lisa. Also found in the hotel are many superb and elegantly displayed antiques, many which are family heirlooms.   The hotel has only twenty-eight rooms, which are always occupied.   I was only able to see one of the rooms, but the one I saw was delightful with exquisite antique beds and a beamed ceiling. Some of the guest rooms have balconies overlooking a charming garden.   I cannot describe the others, and the manager said that each one is different; however, with the excellent taste shown in the lounges and dining room, I imagine that all of the rooms are pleasing.

The Monna Lisa, at one time, was an elegant Renaissance Palace and you will certainly feel like nobility when you are her guest!

PENSIONE MONNA LISA
Owner: Ciardi-Dupre
Borgo Pinti 27
50121 Florence, Italy
tel: (055) 247 9751   telex: 573 300
28 rooms - moderate - great value
5 minute walk from heart of Florence
Exceptionally delightful small inn

The Regency is located on a small park-like square only a ten minute walk from the heart of Florence.   It is however, a world away in atmosphere - instead of the noise of motorcycles and the bustle of tourist-filled streets, you have a peaceful, quiet, elegant setting.   The mood of being "away from it all" is enhanced as you enter the hotel.   Again you are protected.   The front door is usually kept locked and only guests of the hotel are allowed inside.   You ring the front door bell just as you would in a private home.   Although small, the Regency is a deluxe hotel and, in fact, it is quite amazing that with only twenty-eight rooms the Regency can offer so many of the luxuries that are usually found only in larger hotels, such as a concierge to assist you with any of your personal needs and an intimate restaurant in a gorgeous wood panelled dining room.

The bedrooms are spacious and luxurious with excellent lighting and elegant bathrooms.   I would prefer a few more antiques, but these are found mostly in the lounges and the dining room.   At the present time, the Regency spreads into two adjacent "homes" with a garden connecting the wings.   I understand that another home has been purchased so that more guest rooms can be added.

HOTEL REGENCY
Owner: Amedeo Ottaviani
Piazza Massimo d'Azeglio, 3
50121 Florence, Italy
tel: (55) 245 247   telex: 571058
28 rooms - very expensive

As an alternate to staying in downtown Florence, you might want to consider instead the Villa La Massa which is located on the banks of the Arno about a fifteen minute drive from town.   The Villa La Massa is actually composed of three buildings - each old and each having its own unique charm.   This beautiful estate originally belonged to the rich and powerful Giraldi family.   Tombstones with inscriptions, underground tunnels and a chapel still remain from this period of the villa's ancient history.

Although the Villa La Massa is very old, the hotel offers all of the modern ammenities including tennis courts, a swimming pool, air conditioning, refrigerators in the guest rooms, and a choice of restaurants.   One of the restaurants, the Fusica, is very elegant and located in what used to be the dungeon.   The other, the Candele, is light and airy and has a beautiful terrace for outdoor dining.

If you have a car, then the Villa La Massa might make an appealing alternate to staying in the heart of Florence.   Especially in summer when you can do your sightseeing during the day and return to a pool and garden setting at night.

HOTEL VILLA LA MASSA
Manager: C. Manetti
50010 Candeli, Florence
tel: (55) 630051 telex: 573555
40 rooms - very expensive
15 minute drive east of Florence
Located on bend of Arno River
Swimming pool,   tennis courts

The Villa Villoresi is located on a hillside to the north of Florence. It is a wonderful bargain for those who enjoy the atmosphere of a great old villa without paying a fortune. It seems incredible, but you can stay at the Villa Villoresi with meals for less than room alone would cost at most hotels in the heart of town. At one time the Villa Villoresi must have been absolutely gorgeous with its painted ceilings, Venetian glass chandeliers, porticoed balconies, and antique furnishings. The grandeur has faded a bit, as has the neighborhood, but some things never change, and once you are settled in this lovely villa you quickly forget that the neighborhood is not as pristine as it used to be and that the interior is slightly shabby. In fact, in the evening as you sit in the garden by the pool, sharing your day's adventures with other guests, you will think this hillside oasis is perfection.

The Villa Villoresi's greatest asset is Contessa Cristina Villoresi, who owns and manages the hotel. The villa has been in her family since the 19th century and only recently has been converted into a hotel. Countess Villoresi's warmth and graciousness makes everyone feel like a very special guest in a private home.

VILLA VILLORESI
Contessa Cristina Villoresi
Colonnata di Sesto Fiorentino
50019, Florence, Italy
tel: (55) 4489 032
30 rooms - moderate, good value
Excellent hotel for families
Lovely pool in garden setting
Suburb on hill NW of Florence

It would be difficult to find another hotel with as many attributes as the Villa San Michele. In fact, almost impossible. How could one surpass a wooded hillside setting overlooking Florence, a stunning view, gorgeous antiques, impeccable management, gourmet dining, and, as if this were not enough, a building designed by Michelangelo!

The Villa San Michele originally was a monastery whose inner courtyard dates back to the 15th century.   No expense has been spared in the reconstruction of this fabulous building to maintain the ancient ambiance.   There are only thirty-two guest rooms, and although not large, they are decorated with elegant taste. The lounges, dining rooms, terraces, and gardens are also exquisite.   Breakfast and either dinner or lunch are compulsory, but this is no problem since the food is delicious.   There is a beautiful dining room inside or a balcony stretches along the outside of the building where meals are also served.   A pool is scheduled soon to be completed on a terrace above the hotel. Surely, like everything else at this hotel, it will be perfectly delightful.

VILLA SAN MICHELE
Via Doccia, 4, Fiesole
50014, Florence, Italy
tel: (055) 59451 telex 570643
32 rooms - VERY expensive
Open end of March to mid Oct

Credit cards: AX and VS
Designed by Michaelangelo
Luxury hotel NE Florence

The Pensione Baia D'Oro was a discovery.   We had stopped for some coffee in Villa Gargnano and while enjoying the view noticed a picture perfect little pier complete with jaunty, gay umbrellas just north of the village square.   Walking over to investigate we found a cozy restaurant, tiny bar and a small lounge with lots of copper on the walls.   The dining room doors opened out onto the sun filled deck extending over the lake which we had been admiring from a distance.

Mrs. Terzi, the owner's wife, greeted us most cordially.   This is another one of the family owned small hotels whose charm and special character are definitely the imprint of very personalized management.   Although not a fancy hotel by any means (in fact rated a third class pensione by the government) this little inn definitely has a wealth of attributes frequently not found in larger hotels of much higher rating.   The menu is extensive and specializes in pastas and fish dishes.   The bedrooms are simple, but all have private bathrooms.   And there is another interesting touch.   The owner, Gianbattista Terzi, is a famous artist whose paintings hang in many of the galleries of Europe giving the inn an extra bonus of being an art gallery with his paintings adorning the walls.

Pensione Baia D'Oro
Family Terzi
25084 Villa di Gargnano
Lake Garda, Italy
tel: (0365) 711 71
14 rooms - inexpensive
Open Mar 15 - Oct 31
Lovely terrace on the lake
On west shore of Lake Garda

Although the Pensione Giulia is considered a third class pensione by the government - partially I am sure because there are no private bathrooms - it is a wonderful "budget" hotel.   Frequently budget hotels lack charm and location, but not the Pensione Giulia.   The inn is a superb old Victorian looking villa in a large park which extends down to Lake Garda.   The dining room which is on the reception level is beautiful with enormous chandeliers and lovely antique style chairs.   And best yet, Signora Bombardelli, the owner, is usually bustling about in the kitchen overseeing personally the preparation of the next meal.   Up a dramatic staircase are the bedrooms with large French style beds and armoirs. Although the curtains and other details of the bedrooms' decor do not live up to the expectations of the wonderful furniture, who can complain when the view is out across the garden to the shimmering blue lake?   There is another dining room on the garden level of the hotel which opens out to the terrace where more tables are set for dining.   This dining room is much more modern and does not have the ambiance of the more formal dining room upstairs.

The Pensione Giulia is definitely a very simple hotel, but for those who want old world ambiance and a great location combined with a budget hotel, this is an excellent choice.

PENSIONE GIULIA
Family Bombardelli
25084 Gargnano
Lake Garda, Italy
12 room - inexpensive - budget
Lakefront Victorian style villa
Located west shore Lake Garda

The Villa Fiorio is located about fifteen miles south of Rome near the hilltown of Frascati which has always been a favorite playground of the Romans.   It might be an especially good choice of a hotel if you are flying into Rome and do not want to drive too far your first day.   The villa is located on the main highway which runs between Frascati and Grottaferrata.   Although the street is right in front of the hotel, there are gardens to either side of the hotel and a lovely lawn with trees in the rear.   Among the olive trees to the right of the hotel is a beautiful large swimming pool.   Here you can enjoy a country ambiance very close to Rome but at a fraction of the Rome hotel prices!

The Villa Fiorio was built as a summer home for a wealthy Italian doctor and the interior is quite ornate with fancy Italian furniture, lots of mirrors, gilded tables, and elaborate wall sconces.   Upstairs the bedrooms continue the ornate motif.   In the reception hall there are slides of the various bedrooms showing each unique decor so that if space is available, you can choose the room that most appeals to your particular taste!

VILLA FIORIO
Owner: Pierino Maccari
Viale Susmet 25
00046 Grottaferrata, Italy
tel: (6) 945 9276
20 rooms - moderate
Old villa set in garden
Beautiful swimming pool
15 miles south of Rome

The Villa La Principessa is a lovely old mansion surrounded by beautiful gardens. In a parklike setting behind the hotel is a large swimming pool with lounge chairs and umbrellas for relaxing in the sun.   In the distance are lush, green hills.   The entire effect is refreshing and serene.   Unfortunately the interior of the villa does not maintain the same degree of quiet elegance as does the exterior.   The entry hall has some lovely antiques and a beautifully panelled ceiling, but the carpet is a loud plaid which would be better suited for a Scottish castle.   In one of the lounge rooms, the carpet is purple and the walls and draperies a bright green.   The bedrooms, too, are decorated in bright colors.   The dining room, however, tones down and is quite charming.

This is an expensive, well maintained, luxury hotel.   Although the decor is rather bright, I think those of you looking for a stopover near Pisa will find this definitely the best choice.

HOTEL VILLA LA PRINCIPESSA
55050 Massa Pisana
Lucca, Italy
tel: (583) 370 037   telex: 590068
44 rooms - expensive
Closed December to late February
Credit cards: all major

On road leading north from Pisa
About 45 miles west of Florence

The Hotel Santavenere was a wonderful surprise. I had seen pictures of the hotel before I arrived and it looked rather like a motel - a long narrow building with each floor a row of guest rooms.   The photographs did not do it justice. The hotel is absolutely a knockout!   From the moment you walk into the lobby, the gracious ambiance of an exquisite country home surrounds you.   The living room is elegant, but not "stuffy."   Soft comfortable sofas and lounge chairs slipcovered in an attractive country print form cozy conversation nooks. Excellent antiques lend further charm.   Plus, there are many nautical accents, such as delightful models of sailboats, giving even more interest to the room. The dining room follows in excellent taste - a large airy room with highbacked wooden chairs, fresh flowers on the tables, and white linen cloths.   The bedrooms are beautifully decorated with excellent copies of antiques and have beautiful modern bathrooms.   Each bedroom opens onto its own terrace or balcony with lovely sea views.   The location too is exceptional. The back of the hotel drops down a steep wooded hillside, but there is a beautiful green lawn adorned with a swimming pool which stretches to the side of the hotel.   Beyond the lawn the cliffs drop suddenly to the sea and a small private pier.

HOTEL SANTAVENERE
85040 Maratea, Italy
tel: (973) 876 160
44 rooms - expensive
Open June to Sept 26
All room rates MAP
Credit cards: VS, AX, DC
About 130 miles south Naples
On the sea, Pool, tennis

Once in a while a hotel is so perfect that it is tempting not to include it - selfishly fearful that if everyone knows how exceptional it is there might not be "room in the inn" when we return.   The Castel Freiberg is just that special, but conscience dictates sharing with you our Shangri La.   This fantasy castle cresting a hilltop in the mountains near Merano exudes charm.   All of the public rooms are a decorator's dream where priceless antiques abound.   The bedrooms each individual in decor are all tastefully furnished and some have balconies overlooking the mountains.   Even if the setting were not perfect, this castle would be a "winner" because of its enchanting decor, but add to this a gorgeous restaurant in a richly panelled room with gourmet cooking and what else could you possibly desire?   Well, there is more.   If you talk to the masterful and professional concierge, Wolters Siegrid, you will find that surrounding the Castel Freiberg is a maze of splendid walking paths. Also, of course, there is a beautiful pool in a garden setting with the Dolomites as a dramatic backdrop.   As well as an inside pool, c'ay tennis courts, an excercise room, and more - you must go to see for yourself!

HOTEL CASTEL FREIBERG
Owner: Family Bortolotti
39012 Merano, Italy
Tel: (0473) 441 96   telex: 401081
27 rooms - expensive
Credit cards: AX; Open Easter-Oct

Near Merano in Northern Italy
2 Pools, tennis, children's play yard

Schloss Labers is a lovely old castle which dates back to the 11th century.   It has a picturesque setting on a hillside surrounded by vineyards and overlooking the beautiful Adige Valley which is framed by dramatic mountains.   Although not luxurious, this castle has character and charm.   Probably its major attribute is excellent management by the Stapf-Neubert family who oversee every detail of the operation and take personal responsibility to insure that everyone is properly pampered.   I spoke to Mr. Neubert who told me that his grandfather came from Copenhagen in 1885, bought the castle which became so popular with his visiting friends that it soon became a prosperous hotel.

The lounges and dining rooms are not fancy, but have a lived in, comfortable ambiance.   The central staircase dramatically leads upstairs where there are thirty-five bedrooms - many with lovely mountain views.   The setting of this old castle is peaceful and quiet, and if you enjoy being in the countryside, there is a marvelous network of walking paths leading in every direction.

HOTEL CASTEL LABERS
Owner: Family Stapf-Neubert
Via Labers 25
39012 Merano, Italy
tel: (473) 344 84
35 rooms - moderate
Open end March to November
Credit cards: AX, DC, MC
Overlooks valley and mountains
Mountains in Northern Italy
Swimming pool-good for families

If you love picturesque chalet-style hotels in quiet, isolated surroundings, then the Hotel Vigiljoch will definitely be your cup of tea. There is absolutely no highway noise. There are no cars! The only way to reach the hotel is by cable car which you take from the town of Lana which is near Merano in the mountains of northeastern Italy.

The cable car rises quickly from the floor of the valley and has a breathtaking view of the vineyards and apple orchards. When the cable car reaches the top and slowly joggles into the terminal you will see the Hotel Vigiljoch just to the left of the station. In summer, flowers will be bursting from every window and umbrellas will be gaily decorating the front terrace. Inside you will find quite simple bedrooms, but many of which have balconies with a sweeping view of valley and mountain. The bedrooms are small but pleasantly furnished with furniture painted in an Alpine motif. A sprinkling of antiques highlight the lounges. My very favorite room is an intimate, wooden-panelled dining room whose wonderful country prints of blue and red mingle with delightful, light, wooden furniture.

HOTEL VIGILJOCH
1-39011 Vigiljoch
Lana bei Merano, Italy
tel: (473) 512 36
Open Jun-Oct, Dec 20-Apr 20
41 rooms - inexpensive
Pool, Mountain top setting
Accessible only by cable car
Near Merano in Northern Italy

The Hotel Marino alla Scala is a superbly located small hotel.   For opera lovers, the location is more than perfect as it shares the same small piazza with what is probably the world's most famous opera house, La Scala.   For shoppers the location is fantastic because just steps away is the romantic domed arcade of elegant shops and lovely sidewalk cafes.   As you leave the beautiful pedestrian arcade you find yourself facing the awe inspiring Milan cathedral with its incredible array of spires reaching into the sky in a lacey pattern.   However, the Marino alla Scala has much more going for it than just location.   At first glance the hotel seems rather ordinary, but if you are a guest, the merits of the hotel are apparent.   Although the bedrooms are simple, they are immaculately clean and expertly serviced.   The lounges have more charm with crystal chandeliers and some antiques.   What really won my heart is a cozy little bar with a minute staircase leading to a romantic little alcove!   There is no dining room, however, with a wide selection of restaurants within steps of the hotel this certainly poses no problem.

The Marino alla Scala is not inexpensive, yet compared to the large deluxe hotels it is a wonderful "buy."   In fact it is so popular among knowledgeable tourists that rooms are always at a premium so be sure to book far in advance.

HOTEL MARINO ALLA SCALA
Piazza della Scala, 5
20121 Milan, Italy
tel: (2) 867 831   telex: 312680
79 rooms - expensive - good value
Excellent central location
Adjacent to Alla Scala Opera

Of course, it is fun to be in the heart of Venice, but for half the price of what you would pay for a first class hotel there, you can stay twenty minutes to the north at the Villa Condulmer, a splendid 17th century villa whose rooms more closely resemble a museum than a hotel. The rooms are grand with fabulous wall frescoes painted by Moretti Laresi.   The eight rooms in the original villa are the most sumptuous in decor, however in the heat of summer you might prefer the newer wing whose rooms provide the option of air conditioning.

There are several lovely dining rooms for you to enjoy.   In addition, when the weather is balmy, you may choose to have your meals served outdoors on the terrace.   In the garden is a large pool and nearby a gym set which would appeal to children.   For adult "play", there is a golf course adjacent to the hotel where arrangements can be made for you to play if you have a letter of introduction from your club in the United States.   Should you like horseback riding this too can be arranged.

VILLA CONDULMER
1021 Mogliano Veneto,
Italy
tel: (41) 457 100
33 rooms - moderate
Open April - October
Credit cards: AX, DC, MC
12 miles north of Venice
Pool, tennis, play yard
Good stopover for children

Hotel Bewallerhof is not a luxury hotel, but it is truly my dream of everything an idyllic mountain inn should be!   A cozy farmhouse chalet, tucked into a remote mountain valley, a meadow of green velvet stretching out in front to a far vista of beautiful mountains peaks, spectacular giant walls of granite forming the backdrop, wild flowers in the fields, cows munching grass in the distance, birds singing, walking trails spider-webbing out in every direction,   pleasant decor, good food, and a large deck to enjoy a fabulous view.   The Bewallerhof has it all. Even with excellent maps, the inn is extremely tricky fo find.   Although finding it is half the fun, I will give you a few hints.   The Bewallerhof is located between the towns of Eggen (also called Ega) and Obereggen (also called San Floriano.)   If you are driving from Bolzano head southeast through the Val d'Ega for approximately ten miles watching for the turn to the right for Obereggen.   If you arrive at Nova Levante, you have gone too far so turn back and ask directions.   Should you be coming from Cortina, then follow the "Old Dolomite Road" west from Cortina watching carefully for the turn off toward Nova Levante.   When you reach Nova Levante it is only about three miles until you reach the road to the left for Obereggen.   These general instructions should help you in pin pointing the town on your own detailed map.

HOTEL BEWALLERHOF
Proprietor: Family Eisath
39050 Obereggen (San Floriano), Italy
tel: (0471) 615 729
21 rooms - inexpensive - great value
Open Jul-Oct 15 and Dec 20-Apr 10
Old farmhouse in fabulous setting
Dolomites, about 15 miles SE Bolzano

The Gasthof Obereggen is probably one of the simplest inns included in this guide, but it is quite wonderful.   The inn is located overlooking a gorgeous mountain valley in one of the most beautiful mountain regions of Northeastern Italy.   The town of Obereggen is a ski resort and the lift is just a few minutes walk from the hotel.   From the sun soaked deck which extends generously out from the hotel, there is an absolutely glorious vista across the green meadows to the mountains.   Behind the hotel even more majestic mountains poke their jagged peaks into the sky.

Inside there is a cozy dining room.   Mr. Pichler must be a hunter for trophies line the walls.   There is a typical tiled stove against one wall to keep the room toasty on a cold day.   The inn has twenty-five bedrooms; none with private bath but those on the second floor open out onto lovely view balconies.   The greatest asset of this inn, and the real reason for its inclusion, is Mrs. Pichler.   She is just very special - running her little inn with such a warmth and gaiety that just being in the same room with her is fun.   Mrs Pitchler speaks no English, but her hospitality crosses all language barriers, and her abundant and delicious "home style" cooking speaks to all who love to eat!

GASTHOF OBEREGGEN
Owner: Family Pichler
39050 Obereggen (San Floriano)
Italy
tel: (0471) 615 722
25 rooms - inexpensive - budget
Simple inn, wonderful hospitality
Dolomites about 15 miles SE Bolzano

The town of Orvieto, just off the main expressway between Rome and Florence, is one of the most picturesque of all the Umbrian hilltowns and makes an excellent stopover.   An added attraction of Orvieto is staying at La Badia, truly a sightseeing destination in itself!   The hotel, which is located in the rolling hills beneath Orvieto, is actually a 12th Century monastery.   Here you will be treated to a wonderful castle-type atmosphere and will be surrounded by the romantic remains of a marvelous old Gothic abbey.

The dining room is especially wonderful with its enormous high ancient stone vaulted ceilings, its wrought iron fixtures, some heavy wooden beams, the eye-catching copper accents and, at one end, its cavernous fireplace complete with a spit for roasting over the open fire.   The bedrooms are not large, but are pleasant and many have a stunning view of the town of Orvieto.

In the meadows behind the monastery there is a pool which makes a welcome respite from a day on the road.   Children will find both the large pool and the "castle" look of the hotel especially enjoyable.

LA BADIA
05019 Orvieto Scalo
Italy
tel: (763) 90 359
24 rooms - moderate
Credit cards: all major
About 3 miles south of Orvieto
Hotel built into ancient abbey
Pool, tennis, good for children

This wonderful hotel was once the home of the famous Tuscan family, Della Robbia.   Today the villa belongs to the Duchess Visconti who, although she is in her eighties, comes frequently to the villa to insure that her impeccable standards and exquisite taste prevail.   Staying at the Villa le Barone is a dream-like experience, very much like being the fortunate guest in a private, elegant home set in the gorgeous Tuscany hills.

There are only twenty-five guest rooms here, all of which vary in size and decor, but each with an individual charm.   In addition, there is a lovely pool on a terrace overlooking the vineyards and out to the mellow hills beyond. Wonderful little terraces are found secluded in the park-like setting where guests can find a quiet nook to read or just to sit and soak in the beauty.   The food is divine and in balmy weather lunch can be taken in the garden and dinner perhaps inside in a charming dining room which formerly housed the stables. Reservations are accepted for a minimum of three night's, but that should be no problem - three nights will be too short an interlude to spend in this romantic paradise!

VILLA LE BARONE
Owner: Caterina Buonamici
Via San Leolino, 19
50020 Panzano in Chianti, Italy
tel: (55) 852 215
25 rooms - moderate
Minimum stay 3 days
Open Easter through October
Tuscany villa south of Florence

How smug I felt at "discovering" the Castel Pergine for here is a picturebook castle perfect for the budget minded tourist.   No need to forfeit romance and glamour for even though the Castel Pergine is inexpensive, it has a fabulous location dominating a hilltop above the town of Pergine. Luckily, this castle has been delightfully transformed into a small hotel with incredible views out over the valleys and wooded hills.   From the tower you can even see two small lakes in the distance inviting a picnic.

The Castel Pergine is far more famous as a restaurant than a hotel (Michelin gives the kitchen a two fork rating!)   The dining room has a wonderful medieval decor, gorgeous views, and delicious food.   There are, however, a few simple bedrooms.   The ones I saw were somewhat camp-like with basic beds, a wash basin, and a chest of drawers.   None of the rooms had private bathrooms, although there are, of course, facilities on each floor.   But for the price conscious the total ambiance of this castle in the sky is worthy of any budget itinerary - especially if you are with children who will love their personal Disneyland-like castle.

CASTEL PERGINE
Owner: Family Fontanari
38057 Pergine, Italy
Tel: (461) 531 158
12 rooms-inexpensive, budget
Open May to October
Ancient castle - lovely views
North - 7 miles west of Trent
Excellent for children

I am such a romantic that, as the boat chugged across the lake from Stresa to the medieval fishing village of Isola Pescatori and I saw the Albergo Verbano with its reddish-brown walls, dark green shutters, and tables set on the terrace overlooking the lake, my heart was won - completely! On entering, the lobby has rather lumpy, worn furniture; however, the room then opens onto a very nice dining room whose arched windows overlook Lake Maggiore. A second dining area is set up on the terrace with romantic views of the lake. Upstairs the twelve bedrooms vary considerably. One I saw was quite drab but another was very charming with its painted furniture.

The Hotel Verbano has a marvelous restaurant. The gourmet cook has been at the Verbano creating culinary delights for the guests of Hotel Verbano for twenty-eight years; now that is really a record! So that you can sample some of her marvelous pasta, do hurry before she retires. If you desire a reasonably priced hotel, one that is perhaps a little shabby but exudes local color, by all means try the Verbano! I do not believe you will be disappointed.

HOTEL VERBANO
Owner: Family Facchera
28049 Isola dei Pescatori
Borromee Isole
Lake Maggiore, Italy
tel: (323) 30 408   telex: 200396
12 rooms - inexpensive
Open Mid April to October
Lovely lake front restaurant
Island in Lake Maggiore

The Relais El Toula is a tiny, eight room, super deluxe, exquisite inn located less than an hour's drive north of Venice.   Just to be included in the elegant "Relais et Chateaux" hotel association almost automatically means a divine hotel.   The Relais El Toula is not only a member of this of this prestigious family of hotels, but also is also rated one of their most deluxe hotels in Italy.

The villa has an idyllic, country setting. The original villa is flanked by two arcaded wings which stretch to the sides giving the building an elegant, long, low image.   After driving through the vineyards you arrive at an iron gate through which you enter into a courtyard and the hotel.   Inside there is an abundance of fresh flowers in the lounges and delightful bedrooms.   In addition to the lovely park-like setting and the beautiful rooms, there is another bonus - the food and wines are superb!   It is not surprising that the hotel is so exceptional for it is owned by Alfredo Beltrame, a real pro in the inn keeping profession.   He is the founder of the Toula hotel chain.

RELAIS EL TOULA
Owner: Alfredo Beltrame
Via Postumia, 37
31050 Ponzano, Italy
tel: (422) 96023   telex: 410005
8 rooms - very expensive
Credit cards: AX

About 45 minutes north of Venice
Lovely villa, own vineyards, pool

The Il Pellicano has been beautifully designed in the traditional villa style and, although not old, looks like it has snuggled on the hillside overlooking the Mediterranean for many years. The facade is of stucco, painted a typical Italian russet and set off by a heavily tiled roof. Vines enwrap the building, further softening its effect. One enters the bright lobby whose white walls, wooden beamed ceilings, gay sofas, antique accents, and enormous displays of fresh flowers enliven every conceivable nook and cranny. The overall impression is one of light and color - and great taste!

Beyond the reception area is an outdoor dining terrace. As the terrace extends down the hillside, there is a beautiful pool romantically perched at the cliff's edge. From the pool a staircase leads to a pier at the water's edge. Along this path, small individual terraces with lounge chairs and mats for sunning have been built into the rocks. In front of the hotel is a tennis court, again surrounded by flowers.

IL PELLICANO
Managers: Ennio & Nadia Emili
58018 Porto Ercole, Italy
tel: (564) 833 801   telex: 500131
31 rooms - very expensive
Credit cards: AX, DC

Superb cliff top view location
On coast 96 miles north of Rome

The Hotel Nazionale holds the prime piece of real estate in Portofino; smack in the center of the square overlooking a fascinatingly colorful harbor with its theatrical setting of softly hued houses lining the waterfront, dramatic yachts reflecting in the water, fishing boats drawn up on the shore, ruffian cats meandering about looking for tidbits of fish, and the "jet set" wandering in their expensive clothes through the little boutiques.   All this makes for an exciting and picturesque traveling experience, the kind with which you can readily fill entire photo albums!

It is the location which is so superb about the Nazionale.   But location in Portofino is "what its all about".   The public rooms of the Nazionale border on shabby although by comparison some of the bedrooms are quite nice - especially a few choice rooms which overlook the harbor and have painted Venetian-style furniture. Although some of the rooms are quite small the beds are comfortable. The bathrooms are modern and very good.   If you are willing to sacrifice luxury for the thrill of being "center stage" in one of Italy's most picturesque fishing villages, then the Hotel Nazionale is definitely the supreme choice.

HOTEL NAZIONALE
Owner: Bruno Briola
16034 Portofino, Italy
tel: (185) 691 38
56 rooms - moderate
Breakfast only served
Picturesque fishing village
Main square - by the port
About 22 miles east of Genoa

The Splendido is truly a luxury hotel!   Located up a winding, wooded road high above the town of Portofino, it sits majestically above the beautiful blue Mediterranean and overlooks the boats which are moored in Portofino's lovely harbor.   The hotel is much like a very stately, wealthy country home.   On a terrace below the hotel is an enormous swimming pool.   There is also a tennis court located in the gardens to the left of the hotel.   The public rooms are charming with comfortable chairs covered with floral prints and fresh flowers galore.   There is a delightful outdoor terrace where meals are served.   The bedrooms too are lovely and many have balconies which overlook the sea. There are also romantic little pathways originating from the hotel.   You can stroll the wooded grounds and stop along the way at strategically placed benches to enjoy incomparable views.

The Splendido is deluxe and expensive, but it is a beautiful hotel.   If you love luxury and desire a resort setting in one of the most naturally scenic parts of Italy, you will certainly enjoy the marvelous Splendido.

HOTEL SPLENDIDO
16034 Portofino, Italy
tel: (185) 695 551   telex: 331057
Credit card: All Major
67 rooms - expensive
Two meals a day included in rates
Closed January 7 - March 12
Beautiful swimming pool & tennis
Hilltop setting above Portofino
About 22 miles east of Genoa

Le Sirenuse is a superb luxury hotel tucked smack in the middle of the picturesque ancient fishing village of Positano.   It is no wonder that so many writers and artists have been attracted to this colorful town of brightly hued houses clinging to the precipitous hillside as it drops down to its own small bay. And it is also no wonder that so many of these men of fame have found their way to the oasis of the Le Sirenuse.   From the moment you enter the hotel lobby the mood is set with fresh white walls, tiled floors, oil paintings on the walls, and accents of antiques.   The hotel cascades down the hill and so almost all the rooms capture a wonderful view out over the quaint rooftops and the tiled domed cathedral to the small bay below with shimmering blue water.   It is only a short walk through the perpendicular streets until you are on the beach.

The dining room has walls of glass which allow the maximum enjoyment of the vista below, but most diners prefer the splendor of eating outdoors where the deck is set with tables for dining.   On another level of the hotel there is a small pool for sunning and dipping.

LE SIRENUSE HOTEL
Manager: Luigi Bozza
Via C. Colombo, 30
84017 Positano, Italy
tel: (089) 875 066 telex 770 066
65 rooms - very expensive
Credit cards: AX, VS, DC

Swimming pool - delightful views
Amalfi drive - south of Naples

The Il San Pietro di Positano is touted as one of the most delightful deluxe hotels in the world.   It is.   There is no question about it.   From the moment you approach the hotel "class" is evident.   No large signs.   No gaudy advertising. Just an ancient chapel along the road indicates to the knowledgeable that an oasis is below the hill!   After parking in the designated area near the road, there is a elevator which whisks you down to the lounge and lobby.   You walk out of the elevator to a dream world.   An open spacious world of sparkling white walls, tiled floors, colorful lounge chairs, oriental rugs, antique chests, flowers absolutely everywhere, and arches of glass through which visitas of greenery and sea appear.   To the right is a bar and to the left is a marvelous dining room - again with windows of glass opening to the view, but with the outdoors appearing to come in with the walls and ceilings covered with plants and vines.   The bedrooms too seem to be almost a Hollywood creation - again walls of glass, bathrooms with views to the sea, and balconies on which to sit and dream.   If you can tear yourself away from your oasis of a bedroom, an elevator will whisk you down the remainder of the cliff to the small terrace at the water's edge.   If all this sounds gaudy, it isn't.   It is perfect!

IL SAN PIETRO DI POSITANO
Owner: Carlo Cinque
84017 Positano, Italy
tel: (89) 875 454   telex: 770072
Closed January-March 14
55 rooms - VERY expensive

Credit cards: all major
South of Naples on Amalfi drive

It is no wonder that the Hotel Caruso Belvedere has such an especially spectacular site in Ravello - it was built as a palace in the 11th century by a noble family who probably had their pick of the real estate!   The views of the rugged Amalfi coast from the dining terrace perched high in the clouds is gorgeous.   Many of the bedrooms too have vistas.   Although the decor is not as outstanding as in some of the other hotels in Ravello, the views just can't be surpassed.   If you choose the Caruso Belvedere, splurge and ask for one of their most deluxe rooms.   These are simply decorated and pleasant BUT they also have an enormous balcony which stretches the width of the room to capture again the incredibly romantic coast below.   You will wake in the morning to the sound of birds and the scent of flowers intermixed with the fragrance of the vineyards which drift up from the terraces beneath your balcony.

The Hotel Caruso has more to offer than just its marvelous views.   The dining room offers superb food including a divine specialty of the house - a delicious chocolate souffle which will linger in your memory perhaps as long as the view! The meals are accompanied by wines from their own vineyards. Another real plus is the Caruso family who lovingly and efficiently manage this small hotel.

HOTEL CARUSO BELVEDERE
Owner: Family Caruso
Via Toro, 52
84010 Ravello, Italy
tel: (89) 857 111
26 rooms - moderate
Credit cards: AX
South of Naples, Amalfi Coast

The Marmorata Hotel is cleverly converted from the shell of an old paper mill. Only a few of the old paper mills are still in operation, but at one time the Amalfi area was famous for its production of fine paper.

The official address of the Marmorata Hotel is Ravello, however, it is not located in the cliff town of Ravello, but rather on the coastal highway. As you are driving north from Ravello you will see the sign to the hotel which is snuggled in the rocky cliffs between the road and the sea. As you drive down to the entrance you will note the nautical theme carried throughout the decor from the chairs in the dining room to the mirrors on the walls. The interior is charming with comfortable leather lounge chairs and small oriental rugs. There is a lovely terrace plus on a lower lever snuggled into the rocks a small swimming pool. The bedrooms are small, but nicely decorated, again with the seafaring ambiance. The beds seem to be built into captain's sea chests and nautical prints are on the walls. The bathrooms again are small, but modern and attractive. All of the bedrooms have radios, color television, telephone, air conditioning, and small refrigerators. Many of the rooms have an excellent view of the water and rugged coast.

MARMORATA HOTEL
Strada Statale 163
84010 Ravello, Italy
40 rooms - moderate
Pool, small pier, water front
Lovely views from bedrooms
Converted ancient paper mill
South of Naples - Amalfi Coast

There is something magical about the Hotel Palumbo, a 12th century palace now one of the most special hotels in Italy owned since 1875 by the charming Vuilleumier family.   The location is only perfect - up in the clouds overlooking the terraced vineyards to the brilliant blue sea which dances in and out of the jagged rocky coast.

The Hotel Palumbo is not a deluxe category hotel but what a divine small hotel. The romance begins when you enter the beautiful lobby with with its ancient atrium of arched colonnades, green plants flowing from every nook, masses of fresh flowers and beautiful antiques.   Each small corner is an oasis of tranquility from the tiny bar to the cozy antique filled tiny lounges.   There is a beautiful dining room with a crystal chandelier, bentwood chairs and a fireplace, but usually meals are served on the breathtaking terrace which perches like a bird's nest in the sky.   There is a charming garden in the rear with a vine covered terrace overlooking the Amalfi coast.   Another tiny patio which captures both the sun and the view, is tucked onto the roof of the villa.   There are only twenty bedrooms.   Of these several are in the annex which is located across the street from the villa.

HOTEL PALUMBO
Family Vuilleumier
84010 Ravello, Italy
tel: (089) 857244   telex: 770101
20 rooms - moderate - great value
Credit cards: all major
Old villa - lots of antiques
Delightful hotel - superb views

The Villa Cimbrone is not only a hotel, her gardens are one of Ravello's most famous attractions.   The tourist office proclaims, "the Villa Cimbrone, essence of all the enchantment of Ravello, hangs like a swallow's nest on the cliffs." The villa is reached by a delightful ten minute walk from the main square of Ravello.   The signs are well marked to this favorite sightseeing prize.   Once through the gates, the villa and her magnificent gardens open up like magic. The gardens are truly superb - if you have ever received postcards from Ravello the chances are they showed the view from the terrace of the Villa Cimbrone. Most dramatic of all is the belvedere with its stately Roman statues accenting the dazzling view.   Luckily this outstanding villa is also a small hotel.   The rooms are still of museum quality, even though they do not all have private baths, the furniture is "fit for a king."   The owner, Marco Vuilleumier, gave us a tour of the marvelous old villa which is not open to the public - only to the guests. This fabulous villa was owned by a British Duke, but during the Nazi regime he could no longer hold property in Italy.   So, rather than loose his dream villa the Duke gave it to his agent, Marco Vuilleumier, the present owner.   According to the romantic tale, at the end of World War II, the English nobleman landed with the Allied troops in Salerno and as soon as possible found a jeep and wound up the twisting road to see once again his beloved villa.!

VILLA CIMBRONE
Owner: Marco Vuilleumier
84010 Ravello, Italy
tel: (089) 857 138
20 rooms - moderate
Fantastic gardens & views
Amalfi coast, south of Naples

The Pensione Villa Maria is perhaps best known for its absolutely delightful terrace restaurant which has a bird's eye view of the the magnificent coast. Whereas most of the hotels capture the southern view, the Villa Maria features the equally lovely vista to the north.

Although it is a tiny inn, the Pensione Villa Maria is easy to find because it is on the same path which winds its way from the main square to the Villa Cimbrone. After parking your car in the main square of Ravello, look for the signs toward the Villa Cimbrone.   If you follow the signs along a path through the village you will find in about five minutes the Pensione Villa Maria which is to the right of the path perched on the cliffs.   The building itself is a romantic old villa with a delightful garden restaurant whose view just can't be surpassed.   Inside, there is a cozy dining room and upstairs bedrooms which although simple, all have a private bathroom.   The hotel is owned by the Palumbo family, and another plus is that Mrs Carla Palumbo speaks excellent English should you call for a reservation.   How lucky to be able to have the best of all worlds should you be on a budget - a wonderful view location plus a charming villa.

PENSIONE VILLA MARIA
Carla & Vincenzo Palumbo
Sulla Strada per Villa Cimbrone
84010 Ravello, Italy
tel: (089) 857170 or 857319
7 rooms - Inexpensive - Budget
Wonderful view garden terrace
South of Naples - Amalfi Coast

For those of you who love the enchantment of roaming the lakes by boat and getting the first glimpse of your hotel as the boat glides into port, the Hotel Sole is definitely for you. The Hotel Sole is located on the northern end of Lake Garda in the ancient port of Riva del Garda. Although the city of Riva has mushroomed to accommodate the influx of tourists, the old section which surrounds the harbor has retained a great deal of medieval charm with colorful old buildings, towers, etc.

The hotel is located adjacent to the pier where the ferries dock. At the rear of the hotel an excellent outdoor terrace looks out over the lake and all its activity. The hotel is extremely simple, maybe even slightly run-down, but there is a very lovely atmosphere to the hotel and the location is perfect for those who want to stay in the medieval town of Riva and explore Lake Garda by boat. Its terraces are set with umbrella-canopied tables where one can dine or just enjoy a hot cup of coffee. Who cares if the interior is not a decorator's dream? You will love sitting all day, watching the show as boats of all shapes, sizes, and colors move in and out of this tiny harbor.

HOTEL SOLE
Owner: Antonio Zampiccoli
38066 Riva Del Garda, Italy
tel: (464) 512 686
48 rooms - inexpensive
Open April 10 to October
Credit cards: VS
Next to the ferry landing
North shore of Lake Garda

If exploring ancient ruins and being able to savour the wonders of Rome's Imperial Forum twenty-four hours a day appeals to you, then the Hotel Forum certainly should be your choice for accommodation in Rome.   Even if you do not enjoy archaeological marvels, this is an excellent hotel.   It has so much to offer!   Although it is not, by official ratings, considered a deluxe hotel (which favorably makes it less expensive than some of Rome's "grand" hotels), it is for all practical purposes very deluxe and rich in intimacy and personal charm.

The lobby is more like an exclusive club than a bustling hotel.   Dark, wooden-panelled walls, lush green carpets, beautiful oriental rugs, a cozy bar, and strategically arranged seating for quiet conversation are all available here. The bedrooms are small, but pleasantly appointed; some even offer a great view of the old Roman Forum.   Perhaps the best feature of all though, is the Forum's wonderful rooftop garden restaurant.   Here you can sit in the evening and relax over a leisurely dinner, or, during the day, you can escape from the bustle of the city by taking a quiet lunch while overlooking the fantastic Roman ruins.   What more could one want from a "home away from home" in the romantic city of Rome?

HOTEL FORUM
Via Tor de'Conti 25
00184 Rome, Italy
tel: (6) 6792 446   telex: 622549
81 rooms - expensive
Credit cards: all major
Perfect location for sightseeing
Terrace overlooking Roman Forum

For location, The Gregoriana is superb; it is situated on Gregoriana Street which runs into The Piazza Trinita Dei Monti at the top of The Spanish Steps.   In spite of the perfect location, when I first saw the Gregoriana, I just did not see how I could include it in our "inn" book because it has no antique ambiance; in fact, the decor motif might be classified as Chinese with a touch of art decco!   However, after staying at the Gregoriana, I just did not see how I could not include it.   It is such a unique little inn and has such a sparkle of personality that it brightens the otherwise somewhat impersonal city of Rome.   You will not be just one of thousands of tourists in Rome.   Upon arrival, the concierge will probably already know you by name and will continue to greet you personally as you come and go.   Instead of feeling like a face which goes with a key hanging on the wall, you will feel a warmth and intimacy as if you were a guest in a private home.

The rooms are simple but very pleasant and, like the lobby are decorated with a touch of oriental ambiance. Those at the rear are especially quiet and some enjoy a balcony with a view over the rooftops of Rome.   Only breakfast is served. However, there is a concierge on duty twenty-four hours a day to cater to your special needs.

HOTEL GREGORIANA
Owner: Ernesto Panier-Bagat
Via gregoriana 18
00187 Rome, Italy
tel: (6) 6794 269 or 6797 988
19 rooms - moderate
Breakfast only served
Very personalized service

The Hotel Hassler is a landmark in Rome.   Located on the Trinita Dei Monti Piazza at the top of The Spanish Steps, this small, elite hotel was once a palatial private home.   Its entrance is sedate and elegant.   The reception rooms are a little somber, but this mood is quickly relieved by a perfectly marvelous inner courtyard - a superb little oasis with stone walls covered with vines, statues, flowers, cozy little tables, and a bar.   You can linger in the garden, take a refreshment in the afternoon or perhaps meet a friend for an aperitif in the evening.

The dining room at the Hotel Hassler is also spectacular.   It boasts one of the finest views in Rome.   The entire panorama of the city surrounds you as you dine.   As the evening deepens and the city lights begin to flicker, the scene will become one of romance.

If money is no object, the Hotel Hassler offers some magnificent suites, some with enormous terraces and a view so beautiful that you will be sorely tempted to never set foot from this gorgeous hotel!

HOTEL HASSLER
Manager: R.E. Wirth
Trinita Dei Monti 6
00187 Rome, Italy
tel: (6) 6782 651   telex: 610208
100 rooms - VERY expensive
Credit cards not accepted
Beautiful view restaurant

The outside of the Hotel D'Inghilterra looks hopelessly drab and dingy; in fact, I almost did not venture inside!   But, as you walk in the front door, the mood miraculously improves!   Although some of the furniture needs recovering, there is an ambiance of warmth and dignified charm enhanced by strategically placed antiques, lovely paintings that decorate the walls, some pretty Oriental carpets, antique mirrors and fresh flowers throughout.   Down the hallway is a small bar which seems to be the rendezvous spot for everyone staying at the hotel.   This appealing little bar has beautiful dark wood panelling adorned with colorful prints, intimate little tables, fine antique carpets, and comfortable leather sofas.   The bedrooms are well decorated in traditional decor.

The location of the D'Inghilterra is excellent.   A short walk in one direction will lead you through lovely shopping avenues to the bottom of The Spanish Steps. A short walk in the other direction will lead you to The Trevi Fountain with its hub-bub of activity.

Originally, the Hotel D'Inghilterra was built as a guest house for the famous Torlonia Palace and you will certainly see and appreciate traces of grandeur which are still apparent throughout this once-regal residence!

HOTEL D'INGHILTERRA
Via Bocca di Leone 14
00187 Rome, Italy
tel: (6) 672 161   telex: 614552
102 rooms - expensive
Credit cards: all major
Central location near shopping

The small Hotel Valadier is conveniently located about ten minute's walk from the base of The Spanish Steps and is very near the Piazza Del Popolo where a subway will whiz you to most sightseeing attractions.   The street leading from The Spanish Steps toward the hotel is lined with some lovely antique shops and small specialty stores.   The hotel is located on a tiny, alley-like street off the main thoroughfare between The Spanish Steps and the Piazza Del Popolo.   The outside of the building is plain and unassuming, but inside is a superb hotel for the value it offers.   After looking at hotels in Rome and walking many miles in an attempt to find the best, I discovered most accomodations in the same price category as the Valadier to be dreary and drab.   Neither dreary nor drab the Valadier Hotel is fresh and light, with an abundance of antiques.   The furniture is formal, Italian style, but not heavy nor overwhelming.   The walls are painted in soft pastels.   The bedrooms are simple, but all of them have private bathrooms, and air conditioning is available.   I did not eat at the restaurant, but the dining room looked especially charming.

The Valadier is not a deluxe hotel, but for the price, it is a superb value in the expensive city of Rome.

VALADIER HOTEL
Via della Fontanella, 15
00187 Rome, Italy
tel: (6) 679 6966 or 361 0559
38 rooms - moderate - excellent value
Many ornate antiques in public rooms
Only a few minutes to subway station
10 minute walk to Spanish Steps

San Gimignano is one of the most fascinating of the medieval Tuscany hill towns. Most tourists come just for the day to visit this small town. As you approach this village looks like a city of sky scrapers. Come even closer and the "sky scrapers" emerge as fourteen soaring towers - dramatic reminders of what San Gimignano must have looked like in all her glory when this wealthy town sported seventy-two giant towers! If you are lucky enough to be able to spend the night, San Gimignano has a simple, but very charming hotel, the La Cisterna. The hotel is located on the main square of town and it melts right into the ancient ambiance of the square with its somber stone walls softened by ivy, arched shuttered doors, and red tiled roof. Inside the medieval feeling continues with lots of stone, vaulted ceilings, leather chairs, and dark woods. The bedrooms are not fancy, but pleasant and some have balconies with lovely views of the valley. La Cisterna is probably more famous as a restaurant than as a hotel. People come from miles around because not only is the food delicious, but the dining rooms are delightful. Especially charming is the dining room with the brick wall, sloping ceiling supported by giant beams, and picture windows framing the gorgeous Tuscany hills.

LA CISTERNA
Piazza della Cisterna
53037 San Gimignano, Italy
tel: (577) 940 328
46 rooms - inexpensive
Credit cards: AX, VS
Excellent restaurant
33 miles SW of Florence
Hilltown famous for towers

The Pitrizza is a tiny jewel of a hotel located on the Emerald Coast of the Island of Sardinia - the playground of the Aga Khan and the jet set of of the world. From the moment you enter through the front gate, marked only with a simple little sign, you are in a world of tranquility and beauty.   There is a central clubhouse which has a beautiful lounge, a delightful dining room with hand hewn wooden chairs, a card room, and a bar.   A small protected patio extends from the dining room where meals are served when the weather is warm.   French doors from the lounge open onto the terrace which leads down to a most unusual swimming pool which is cleverly designed into the natural rock.   (The pool is quite wonderful - when in the water the outer edge facing the bay is water level giving the impression that you are in the sea, not in a pool!)   The bedrooms are tucked away in small cottages which blend into the landscape.   The rooms are not especially large but beautiful with every detail of the finest quality.   If your idea of a vacation is a frenzy of activity and "things to do" then the Pitrizza is definitely not for you.   There are no planned activities.   No sports director. No loud music.   Only lovely quiet, gourmet food, a beautiful pool, and a delightful small white sand beach.

PITRIZZA
Manager: Gianfranco Ghione
07020 Porto Cervo, Sardinia, Italy
tel: (789) 92000   telex 790037
28 rooms - VERY expensive
Credit cards: all major
Open May through September

Pool, beach, tennis available

Having heard about a lovely little chalet tucked amidst the pines high in the mountains near the French border, I was beginning to wonder what awaited me as the road wound through the ski town of Sauze d'Oulx with its unattractive jumble of modern concrete ski hotels.   However, the road soon left the resort town and continued twisting higher and higher into the mountains until suddenly the Il Capricorno came into view nestled in the forest to the left of the road!   Just as you enter there is a tiny bar, and beyond, a cozy dining room enhanced by dark wooden chalet style chairs, rustic wooden tables, and a stone fireplace whose wood is stacked neatly by its side.   There is not a hint of elaborate elegance - just a simple cozy country charm.   The perfect kind of inn to come "home" to after a day of skiing or walking the beautiful mountain trails.

The bedrooms too are simple but most pleasant with dark pine hand made furniture neat little bathrooms, and for a lucky few, balconies with splendid mountain views.   However, the greatest asset of this tiny inn are the owners, Mariarosa & Carlo Sacchi.   Carlo personally made most of the furniture and will frequently join the guests for skiing.   Mariarosa is the chef, and a fabulous, gourmet cook.   This is a very special little hideaway for very special people.

IL CAPRICORNO
Mariarosa & Carlo Sacchi
10050 Sauze D'Oulx, Italy
tel: (122) 852 73
Jun 15-Sep 15 & Oct 15-May
8 rooms - inexpensive
Tiny inn - very personalized
Mountain setting near France

The location of the Grand Hotel dei Castelli is fabulous - high on a hill overlooking not one, but two little bays.   In fact, the hotel dominates the entire peninsula and has a spectacular panoramic walk carved along the cliffs as they circle the parklike grounds.   The views to the crashing surf below are breathtaking.   (If you are with children, hold their hands tightly because there is a perilous drop off with only a small guard rail for protection.)   In spite of this great location I contemplated not including the hotel because, although it just verges on greatness, it somehow misses - due I think to a feeling that the property is not well maintained.   However, the hotel has an absolutely divine outdoor dining terrace which outweighs the lack of perfection in other areas. On summer nights when the weather is balmy, tables are set out on a balcony which overhangs the side of the cliff and has an incredibly stunning view of the harbour with its yachts and colorful fishing boats.   This terrace is surrounded by trees, so the effect is one of being suspended in air in a tree house with a view of the sea.   The food is marvelous and the service friendly and professional.   As you linger through a delicious meal of fresh fish and watch first the sunset and then the lights across the bay slowly twinkling on, you will probably think the hotel is perfect!

GRAND HOTEL DEI CASTELLI
16039 Sestri Levante, Italy
tel: (185) 410 44
45 rooms - expensive
Credit cards: all major
Open May 15 to Oct 10
Riviera, 30 miles east Genoa
Natural pool in ocean

Although the Berghotel Tirol is a new hotel, it happily copies the typical chalet style of the Dolomites.   Inside too, the tasteful decor follows the delightful Alpine motif with light pine furniture, baskets of flowers, and a few antiques for accent pieces.   However, what is so very special about the Berghotel Tirol is its marvelous location on a hillside looking over the lovely village of Sexten and to the fabulous mountains beyond.   Many of the rooms have large balconies which capture the view and the warmth of the mountain sun.

The Berghotel Tirol is not actually in the town of Sexten (sometimes called Sesto on the maps), but in a suburb called Moos.   This is one of the most scenic areas of the Dolomites and the town of Sexten one of the most attractive of the mountain towns.   In addition to the natural beauty, there is a wonderful network of trails leading in every direction to tempt all into the crisp mountain air.   When you return at night to the hotel it is rather like a house party.   Most of the guests come for at least a week and table hopping is prevalent as the knicker clad guests share their day's adventures.   Acting as hosts to the "house party" are the extremely gracious, cordial owners, the Kurt Holzer family, who seem to be dedicated to seeing that everyone has a good time.

BERGHOTEL TIROL
Family Kurt Holzer
39030 Sexten (Sesto), Italy
tel: (0474) 70386
30 rooms - moderate
Dec 20-Apr 26 & May 20-Oct
Beautiful mountain valley
Dolomites - near Austria

The Villa Igiea Grand Hotel is an oasis of blissful tranquility in the midst of the large and rather unattractive city of Palermo. With all the fabulous archaeological sites and marvelous cathedrals in the area it is wonderful to have such a splendid hotel to "come home to" at night. The approach to the Villa is not scenic, but from the moment you enter the gates you are in another world. A world of spacious lobbies, sweeping verandas, formal dining rooms, and spacious, well furnished bedrooms with large modern bathrooms. Many of the bedrooms have private balconies overlooking the gardens to the sea.

The hotel is called a villa, but it is much more like a small deluxe castle which is built right at the edge of the sea. A lovely free form swimming pool fits itself onto a ledge which overhangs the water. Adjacent to the pool the hotel has its very own ancient Greek temple - now how many hotels can top that! The most outstanding attributes of the hotel are the gardens. They envelop the hotel in a nest of beautiful pines and masses of gorgeous flower beds intertwined with twisting pathways. Altogether, a most delightful hotel.

VILLA IGIEA GRAND HOTEL
Salita Belmonte, 1 (Acquasanta)
90142 Palermo, Sicily, Italy
tel: (91) 543 744   telex: 910092
118 rooms - expensive
Credit cards: All Major
Swimming pool, tennis, sea front
Own small Greek temple by the sea
Located on northern coast of Sicily

The San Domenico Palace is a super deluxe hotel cleverly incorporated into what was formerly a Domenican Monastery. Don't let the monastery bit deter you. Absolutely no trace of a life of denial remains. In fact, this is one of the most super deluxe hotels in Italy catering to your every whim. As you enter the hotel the lobby opens onto the core of the hotel, the beautiful arcaded renaissance cloister. Around this inner courtyard the vaulted walkway is now glassed in, but filled with light. Leading off of the courtyard are various lounges, writing rooms, and game rooms. The dining room is a masterpiece. It has high backed wooden chairs, enormous arched windows and a panelled ceiling. The chapel has been converted into a bar. Throughout the hotel there are priceless antiques of a quality which would make a museum blush with pride. Many of the bedrooms look out to the beautiful bay of Taormina.

In the rear of the hotel there is a beautiful garden filled with gorgeous flowers. Pathways lead throughout the gardens with small nooks where you can stop to soak in the splendid sea view. A swimming pool is squeezed into the property just as it drops down to the road below. There is no doubt that this is a MOST dramatic hotel.

SAN DOMENICO PALACE
Piazza San Domenico 5
98039 Taormina, Sicily, Italy
tel: (942) 237 01
100 rooms - expensive
Credit cards: all major
Swimming pool - tennis

It is hard to be objective when you are "in love" and I fell in love with the Hotel Timeo from the moment I walked through the front gates and into the garden whose bougenvillia covered trellis covers the pathway to the door.   This is just my kind of hotel, so it is difficult for my personal preferences not to peak through.   The Hotel Timeo is a wonderful old villa.   The same family has owned the hotel for over one hundred years and it still maintains the wonderful quality of a private home - one loved and cherished by the owners.   The lounges and dining room have many lovely antique pieces.   The bedrooms are not outstanding in decor, but splurge and ask for one with French doors opening onto its own patio.   If you are blessed by sunny days and star lit nights you too will surely fall in love!   The view is incredibly lovely.   You look out over the gardens to the shimmering waters far below.   And, in the distance, proudly dominating the horizon is Mount Etna.

Besides being such a lovely hotel, the Timeo is perfectly located.   The town of Taormina is a lovely medieval town loaded with charm, and the main gate is only down a short alley from the hotel.   Behind the hotel, just a short path from the road, is the Greek Theatre, certainly one of the main sights in Taormina.

HOTEL TIMEO
Manager: Loturco Pancrazio
59 Via Teatro Greco
98039 Taormina, Sicily, Italy
tel: (942) 238 01   telex: 980073
55 rooms - moderate
Credit cards: all Major
Closed Nov 11 to Dec 19

The Villa Sant' Andrea is not in the ancient cliff top village of Taormina, but located instead in the village which clusters below. There is a cable car which can whisk you quickly back to Taormina for sightseeing or shopping. The cable car is located only a short block from the hotel so is most convenient. If you are travelling with children the location is especially nice because the hotel is beautifully positioned at the end of a small swimming cove. In fact the property is built in levels which descend right to the beach where the hotel has its own private section for the guests.

You enter the charming old villa from the street level where the reception desk is located. On a lower floor is the dining room which has an informal ambiance with white wicker furniture. The lounge maintains an "English country" look with sofas and chairs upholstered in cheerful floral prints which match the draperies. The bedrooms are simple but many have balconies with beautiful views across the small bay to the dramatic rocks jutting from the brilliant blue water. The hotel was originally built as a private residence for an English family in 1830 and it still maintains the ambiance of an English country estate.

VILLA SANT'ANDREA
Director: Francesco Moschella
98030 Taormina, Mazzaro
Sicily, Italy
tel: (942) 231 25   telex: 980077
36 rooms - moderate
Credit cards: VS, AX
Open April - October
Own private beach

If you would like to combine your sightseeing of Siena with a luxury resort, then the Certosa Di Maggiano might be "just your cup of tea". This is an expensive hotel, but delightful and quite unique. Outside, the hotel looks quite ordinary; just a wall facing the road, but when you step inside it is a fairyland. It doesn't resemble a hotel in the slightest. And it is no wonder! The hotel is built into the restored ruins of a seven hundred year old Carthusian monastery. As you enter the arcaded courtyard you can almost see the ghosts of priests, their dark robes flowing, silently walking beneath the vaulted roof of the cloisters. On three sides of the courtyard are arranged the fourteen guest rooms, the lounges, the game rooms, the library, the bar and the exquisite dining room. The fourth side of the courtyard is formed by a small church.

The guest rooms are spacious and pleasant but not outstanding in decor. However, the public rooms are smashing! Antiques galore, and all of the finest quality. Another bonus. There is a beautiful pool in the gardens which is never crowded since this is such a tiny hotel. In fact, there are so few people around, that it truly is like being a guest in a private estate.

CERTOSA DI MAGGIANO
Manager: Anna Recordati
53100 Siena, Italy
tel: (577)288 180   telex: 574221
14 rooms - Expensive
Credit cards: AX, DC, VS

Swimming pool & tennis courts

A pensione usually means a compromise in accommodations, so what a delightful surprise the Palazzo Ravizza provides. Even though the government has categorized this hotel as a pensione it is, without a doubt, my choice of where to stay in Siena! A 17th Century mansion, the Palazzo Ravizza has belonged to the same family for nearly two hundred years. There are only twenty-eight bedrooms, which definitely vary in quality of decor and location. This is certainly one of the occasions when you will want to request the most deluxe room possible, for, although all rooms are adequate, the ones in the top category are real gems, containing some antique furnishings and possessing lovely panoramic views of the Tuscany hills. The more expensive rooms are also more tranquil since they overlook the garden rather than the street which can be noisy. The Palazzo Ravizza is only a short walk from one of the most gorgeous cathedrals in Italy. It is also only a stroll from the enormous plaza where the running of horses take place. The furniture in the small lounge is comfortable and cozy. The dining room is charming. The total effect is one of the excellent taste and marvelous value. One of the joys of Siena is wandering the intriguing little twisting streets so, although there are several deluxe villa style hotels in the immediate vicinity I would stay right in Siena itself since it has such a lovely small hotel.

PENSIONE PALAZZO RAVIZZA
Plan dei Mantellini 34
53100 Siena, Italy
tel: (0577) 280 462
28 rooms - inexpensive
Located in heart of Siena
40 miles south of Florence

The Locanda dell'Amorosa makes a wonderful base for exploring the hill towns south of Florence.   It is very accessible since it is located in Sinalunga which is just a few minutes from the Expressway between Rome and Florence.   From the Locanda dell'Amorosa it is an easy drive to such sightseeing delights as Siena, Pienza, Orvieto, Todi, and Assisi.   However, it is not location alone which makes the Locanda dell'Amorosa so perfect.   There is far more.   Truly, the Locanda dell'Amorosa would be marvelous if there were nothing nearby.   In fact, the hotel could be a destination in itself!   Actually, this is not a hotel. It is a tiny town a few miles south of Sinalunga.   The approach to "town" is a road lined by a majestic row of Cypress trees.   Park your car and enter the walls of the 14th century medieval town.   You will be greeted by an enormous plaza with its own little church - exquisite inside with its soft pastels and its lovely fresco of the Madonna holding the Christ child.   In the wing to the right are the stables which have been converted to contain a beautiful restaurant.   Heavy beams, natural stone and brick walls are original and are tastefully enhanced by arched windows, thick wrought iron fixtures and wooden tables.   The bedrooms are tastefully appointed with a few antiques and matching bedspreads and draperies. Most guest rooms have peaceful views of forest and soft green hills.

LOCANDA DELL'AMOROSA
Owner: Carlo Citterio
53048 Sinalunga, Italy
tel: (0577) 679 497
7 rooms with bath - moderate
Closed Jan. 20th to Feb. 28th
Credit cards: AX, DC, VS
60 miles south of Florence

As soon as you cross the moat and enter the wonderful medieval village of Sirmione, look to your right.   At the end of the street is an endearing little inn adorned with the Grifone sign.   The outside of the hotel is absolutely charming - a weathered old stone cottage with brown shutters, red-tiled roof, roses creeping up the walls, and a delightful terrace overlooking the lake and castle.

Actually, although they are separate operations, the hotel is in the same building with one of the finest restaurants in Sirmione.   The restaurant is in the front of the house and is oozing with antiques and old world ambiance; it earns its reputation for some of the most delicious cuisine in Sirmione!   The hotel portion of the house has its entrance to the rear and its bedrooms upstairs. Contrary to the marvelous decor of the restaurant, the hotel is absolutely drab. The very simple rooms show no warmth or style, however they each have the luxury of a private bathroom.   Also, although this is a budget hotel, it has a prime Sirmione location.   What is more, if you are lucky enough to get one of the rooms in the front, you will have the added bonus of a little balcony overlooking one of the finest views in town.

HOTEL GRIFONE
Owner: Luciano Maracolini
1-25019 Sirmione
Lake Garda, Italy
tel: (30) 916 014
17 rooms - inexpensive - budget
Dates open: April 20-October
Excellent restaurant in building
Waterfront location on Lake Garda

What a sense of impending grandeur it is to wait for the giant metal gates of the Villa Cortine Palace to swing open.   Once inside the road winds and curves impressively past fountains and statues, flower gardens and mighty trees until you reach the summit where the Villa Cortine Palace reigns.   This beautifully situated villa has been expanded so that the original wing now boasts a new section which appears to have more than doubled the size of the original castle. Some of the remodeling has a "too modern" feel.   One rather wishes that perhaps more of an "olde worlde" ambiance could have been preserved. However, in the old section of the villa, which is to the left as you enter the lobby, the rooms still maintain their grandeur with incredibly ornate furniture, soaring ceilings, and stunning paintings.   Upstairs the guest rooms are large and are decorated with color co-ordinated drapes, chairs, and bedspreads.

What leaves absolutely nothing to be improved upon are the gardens - what a gorgeous sight! In fact, they are absolutely awe-inspiring.   The villa is surrounded by gravelled walkways which wind in and out amongst the fountains, ponds, statues, and glorious rose gardens, all overlooking the lovely lake.

VILLA CORTINE PALACE HOTEL
25019 Sirmione, Italy
tel: (30) 916 021   telex: 300395
54 rooms - expensive
Credit cards: all major

Min. stay 3 days, Open Apr to Nov
Swimming pool, tennis, lake pier
Park setting - overlooks Lake Garda

The Grand Hotel Excelsior Vittoria has a superb location high on the cliff overlooking the port and bay of Sorrento.   One enters the hotel through a formal gate which is just a short stroll from the center of town.   In front of the hotel is a small park-like area with a swimming pool.   The hotel is a grand old villa with a definitely old world atmosphere.   The furnishings, for the most part, continue the antique mood.   The ceilings in some of the reception rooms and in the marvelous airy dining room have gorgeous frescoed designs.   The terraces and gardens surrounding the hotel offer wonderful views, as do the bedrooms which are located facing the bay.

Overall, the hotel has a slightly "worn" look about it but, actually, this fits into the mood of this once magnificent villa.   For those of you who want everything perfect, this would not be the hotel for you, but, in my estimation it is the best in Sorrento.   Splurge here and get one of the superior rooms with a view of the sea.   It will certainly delight anyone who loves the feeling of reliving the grandeur of days gone by in a villa by the sea.

GRAND HOTEL EXCELSIOR VITTORIA
Piazza Torquato Taso 34
80067 Sorrento, Italy
tel: (081) 878 1900 telex: 720368
125 room - expensive
Credit cards: AX, VS
Beautiful views of Sorrento Bay
On cliffs above the harbor
Swimming pool, elevator to harbor
About 30 miles south of Naples

The road to the Pension Stefaner winds up a tiny mountain valley in the heart of the Dolomites.   The road is gorgeous, but extremely narrow and twists like a snake around blind curves whose roadside mirrors are a necessity, not an optional precaution!   As we rounded the last curve before Tiers the valley opened up and there spread before us a sweeping vista of majestically soaring mountains. Across soft green meadows painted with wildflowers and dotted with tiny farm chalets rose an incredible saw-toothed range of gigantic peaks.   Suddenly the journey seemed worth the effort for the scenery alone even if the Pension Stefaner proved to be a disaster.   Luckily though the Pension Stefaner is very nice.   The outside is especially attractive - a chalet with flower laden balconies.   Inside, the inn is a bit too "fussy" for my taste, but the valley is so spectacular that I am sure you will be spending most of your time on the beautiful walking trails which lace the valley.   The Pension Stefaner has some antiques scattered throughout for accents, but the furniture is new. The bedrooms are light and airy and many have balconies.   Although there was no one who spoke English when I was there, friendliness prevailed.   In fact, there was even a gentle, lazy German Shepherd lounging in the lobby offering a friendly welcome.

PENSION STEFANER
Family Stefaner
1-39050 Tiers, Italy
tel: (0471) 642 175
16 rooms - inexpensive
New chalet style inn
Lovely mountain setting
N.E. Italy in Dolomites

Le Tre Vaselle is a very sophisticated inn located in the small wine town of
Torgiano which is very near Assisi.   The decor of the hotel is one of a lovely
country manor.   The owners are the Lungarotti Family, famous for their
production of superb wines.   Mr. Lungarotti owns all of the vineyards around
Torgiano for as far as the eye can see.   The hotel probably evolved to fill the
need for a place for business associates and friends to stay when visiting the
vineyards.   The accommodations are extremely comfortable and have all the
amenities of a large city hotel.   The most amazing aspect of Le Tre Vaselle is
that it has stunning conference rooms furnished in antiques with intimate
adjacent dining rooms.   The Lungarotti family has thought of everything.   To
keep the wives happy, while their husbands are in meetings, the hotel schedules
cooking classes in one of the most professional kitchens I have every seen.   The
Lungarottis also have a private wine museum which would be a masterpiece
anywhere in the world.   Not only do they have an incredible and comprehensive
collection of anything pertaining to wine throughout the ages, but the display is a
work of art.   The museum alone would be worth a detour to the Le Tre Vaselle!

LE TRE VASELLE
Owner: Family Lungarotti
06089 Torgiano, Italy
tel: (75) 982 447   telex: 660189
48 rooms - moderate
Credit cards: AX, DC, VS

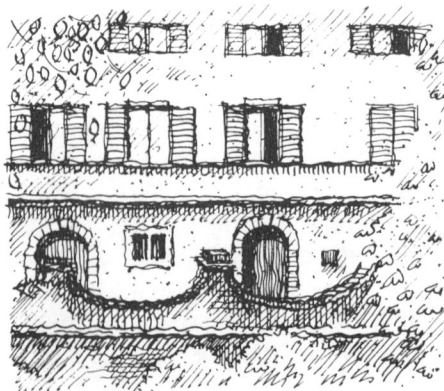

Near Assisi - superb wine museum

The Baia Paraelios is an absolutely delightful hotel tucked onto the spur of land that juts from the toe of Italy near the ancient port of Tropea. The hotel is actually a resort which follows the contours of the hillside from the highway down to the beach. The reception office is located at the top of the hill and the mood is set from the moment you register. The small office is tastefully decorated with plants and charming old prints on the walls and the personnel in the office are gracious and warm in their welcome. The rooms are all bungalows which are artfully terraced down the hill to capture the best view possible from each. Midway down is a lovely pool. At beach level is a beautiful dining room and a comfortable, inviting lounge. The bungalows each have one or more bedrooms, a sitting room, and a deck or patio. The decor is simple but in excellent taste with tiled floors and earth tones used throughout. One of the most beautiful white sand beaches I saw in Italy stretches invitingly in front of the complex. The Bais Paraelios makes a nice stop along your route south. Not only will you have the benefit of a lovely break in your travels, but also the nearby ancient town of Tropea, which hangs on the cliffs above a beautiful bay, is fun to explore.

BAIA PARAELIOS
Proprietor: Adolfo Salabe
88035 Parghelia
Tropea, Italy
tel: (963) 614 50
52 bungalows - moderate
Open May 10 through Sep
Southern Italy-near tip of toe
Pool, tennis, gorgeous beach

The Hotel do Pozzi has a wonderful convenient location down a quiet little pathway off the main walkway which leads from St. Mark's Square.   The hotel has the advantage of being within the heart of Venice and yet in a small world of its own.   Taking full advantage of the sun there is a delighful miniature plaza in a garden setting at the front of the hotel.   Inside, the lobby is pleasantly decorated with a small reception desk, oriental carpets, and some comfortable chairs.   To the left of the lobby is a lounge area and also a delightful small dining room where guests are served breakfast. The bedrooms are simply decorated in a modern motif - nothing special in their decor, but all with private bath.   The bedrooms which face over the little terrace are especially nice.

There is no restaurant in the hotel, but this is not a problem since the excellent restaurant, Raffaele's, which is under the same ownership as the hotel, can be reached by a connecting interior entrance. There is no need to venture outside.

For someone who wants a moderately priced, beautifully located, pleasant hotel which offers a touch of charm, the Do Pozzi makes an excellent choice.

HOTEL DO POZZI
Raffaele, Proprietor
Via XXII Marzo
30124 Venice, Italy
tel:(041) 707855   telex:41275
35 rooms - moderate
Credit cards: AX, VS
Central location on tiny plaza

If you love opulent elegance, and if cost is of no consequence to you, then without a doubt the Gritti Palace will be a perfect choice.   The location is marvelous too - just a short walk from St. Mark's Square yet far enough removed to miss the city's noise and summer mob of tourists.   In fact, with careful planning, you can be entirely insulated in a private and very special world from the moment you arrive until you reluctantly depart.   If you take a private motor launch from the airport or the Piazza Roma, you can stylishly descend at the deluxe little private pier in front of the hotel where porters will be waiting to whisk you to your room where you will be pampered and spoiled.   All at a price, of course.   The Gritti Palace is expensive, very expensive.   But then what would you expect when staying in the 15th century palace of the immensely wealthy Venetian Doge, Andrea Gritti?

The Gritti Palace has a charming terrace on the bank of the Grand Canal where you dine in splendor and watch the constant stream of boat traffic.   The lobby and lounge areas open off of the terrace and are grandly decorated with antiques.   The bedrooms too are large and very fancy in decor, and those that face the canal provide a twenty-four hour show.

HOTEL GRITTI PALACE
Campo S. Maria del Giglio, 2467
30124 Venice, Italy
tel: (041) 26 044   telex: 410125
99 rooms - VERY expensive
Credit cards: All major

The Hotel La Fenice et des Artistes, which absolutely abounds with charm, is a real jewel for Venice.   In fact, it is almost a miracle that in this city of extremely expensive hotels, there is a small, well located inn which sacrifices nothing in ambiance although reasonably priced.

From the moment you enter the Hotel La Fenice et des Artistes you will be entranced.   The lobby is small, but seems spacious since there are two gay little garden patios which open from the lobby.   Here guests sit in the late afternoon for a cup of tea or an aperitif before dinner.   The lobby is a triangle which connects the original building with a newer wing.   Both sections are very nice, although in summer only the newer wing offers the option of air conditioning which can be a blessing on a hot day.   There is a nicely decorated lounge plus a tiny little bar.   The bedrooms are not large, but very pleasant and color coordinated with a different wall paper in each room setting the theme.

Breakfast only is served at the Hotel La Fenice et des Artistes, but this is almost a blessing since within a few blocks there is a wonderful choice of excellent restaurants.

HOTEL LA FENICE ET DES ARTISTES
Dante Appollonio, Manager
Campiello de la Fenice, S. Marco 1936
30124 Venice, Italy
tel: (041) 26 403   telex: 411150
75 rooms - moderate
Excellent value for Venice
Located near La Fenice Theatre

Gourmet Magazine had a superb article on Venice in which they shared several of their favorite little inns.   Except for the article, I probably never would have discovered the Pensione Seguso, since it is off the beaten path - although convenient to the sights of Venice.   The hotel is located on the "left bank" of Venice; in other words, it is across the Grand canal from the heart of the tourist area.   This is no problem because it is only about a fifteen minute walk to St. Mark's Square and even quicker if you hop on the "water bus".

The Pensione Seguso is a simple little inn which has been in the Seguso family for several generations.   They do a marvelous job in providing a homelike ambiance for the guest who does not demand luxury, but appreciates quality.   The delightful surprise is that this hotel has so much to offer.   The location is fun, as it is at the junction of the Giudecca Canal and an intersecting side canal.   In front there is a miniature terrace harboring a few tables set under umbrellas. Several of the bedrooms too have wonderful views of the canal.   The greatest surprise is that the value conscious tourist can stay at the Pensione Seguso with breakfast and dinner included for what the price of a room alone would cost for most hotels in Venice.

PENSIONE SEGUSO
Family Seguso, Proprietors
Grand Canal Zattere, 770
30123 Venice, Italy
tel: (041) 22 340
17 rooms - inexpensive
Rates include two meals a day
Exceptional value for Venice

The Hotel Cipriani was founded by the late Giuseppe Cipriani, who during his lifetime became almost a legend in Venice.   This beloved man, who founded the internationally famous Harry's Bar in Venice, had a dream of building a fabulous hotel within easy reach of St. Mark's Square and yet far enough away to guarantee seclusion and peace.   He bought three acres on the island of Giudecca and with the financial assistance of some of his prestigious friends, such as Princess Brigit of Prussia and the Earl of Iveagh (head of the Guiness brewing company in Dublin), he accomplished his dream - an elegant Venetian palace-style hotel.

The Cipriani is the perfect hotel for those of you who MUST have a pool, for it is the only hotel with a pool in Venice.   And what a pool - it is Olympic size and surrounded by beautiful gardens.   The splendor continues inside where the lounges are tastefully decorated in whites and beiges and the bedrooms are large and elegant.   You truly have the best of all worlds at the Cipriani - you are at a superior resort yet only minutes from the heart of Venice in the private launch which waits to whisk you, any time of the day or night, to St. Mark's Square.

HOTEL CIPRIANI
Manager, Dr. Natale Rusconi
Isola della Giudecca, 10
30123 Venice, Italy
tel: (041) 707 744   telex: 410162
94 rooms - very expensive
Credit cards: AX

If the idea of being close to Venice and yet near a beach and casino appeals to you, then perhaps you should consider a hotel located on the lido, a small island opposite St. Mark's Square.   A fifteen minute boat ride and a short taxi trip brings you to the Albergo Quattro Fontane, a charming inn which reminds me more of a French country home than an Italian villa.   It has a white stuccoed exterior with gabled roof, green shutters, and vines creeping both over the door and around some of the small balconies.   To the left of the main building is a lovely courtyard whose privacy is enhanced by another wing of the hotel giving the garden a cozy, "walled" in effect.   Inside the hotel there is an ambiance of a country home with antiques cleverly used throughout the lounges.

The beach is only a short distance away.   The Albergo Quattro Fontane can make arrangements for you to reserve a private beach cabana when you arrive at the inn.   The cost per day will vary, depending both upon the location and the comparative luxury of the cabana you choose.   The beach is wide and the water clear, although the sand is not as fine and white as many of our American beaches.   Still, it is quite an experience just to sample the interesting hierarchy of the Italian beach system.

ALBERGO QUATTRO FONTANE
Via 4 Fontane
30126 Lido of Venice
Venice, Italy
tel: (041) 760 227
70 rooms - expensive
Open end of Apr to Oct 1
Near casino, beach, tennis

The tiny island of Torcello is located about fifty minutes from Venice by boat. This lovely sleepy little island is usually considered a short stop for the tour boats as they ply their way among the maze of little islands surrounding Venice. But, for those who want to linger on Torcello, where they can be close to Venice yet feel out in the country, there is a deluxe inn which is owned by the Cipriani family. This small inn, the Locanda Cipriani, is well known to knowledgeable gourmets as a fantastic restaurant. Many arrive every day from Venice just to dine, and depart never knowing that upstairs this restaurant also has guest rooms. The inn is very simple, much more like a small farm house than a deluxe hotel. Inside there is a rustic, cozy dining room and outside a beautiful dining terrace surrounded by gardens brilliant in summer with all varieties of flowers. There are only a few bedrooms which are all suites. Breakfast and dinner are included in the room rate. This is an expensive inn, but an elegant hideaway for relaxing and dining royally in a beautiful country setting. Many famous guests have already discovered this oasis - including Hemmingway, who came here to write. I think you will share his belief that the Locanda Cipriani Torcello is a very special place!

LOCANDA CIPRIANI TORCELLO
Proprietor: Family Cipriani
30012 Isola Torcello
Venice, Italy
tel: (041) 730 150
5 suites - expensive
Visa card, Open Mar 19- Nov 10
Luxury inn on quiet little island
Reached by boat from Venice

While visiting the island of Torcello, which is located about fifty minutes from Venice by boat, I noticed a "picture perfect" stone cottage nestled by a tiny canal. The ambiance of this cottage, the Villa '600, reminded me of the French mills which are so appealing. On a terrace by the front entrance diners, obviously enjoying their noonday meal in the sun, were seated at wooden tables covered in checked cloths.   Inside, there was another rustic dining room where seated around one of the tables was a family (complete with a dog on one of the chairs) obviously having a delightful lunch.   Although there was no indication of guest rooms, I felt compelled to inquire in hopes that this idyllic restaurant might also be an inn.   I spoke to Stefano, the handsome director. "No," he said, "we have no bedrooms."   My anticipation melted away until he added, "They are all full."

This tiny isolated inn is only accessible by boat and, unlike some of the other islands surrounding Venice, the schedule is infrequent.   Once you arrive, there are only four very simple bedrooms, and the bathroom is "down the hall." However, the setting is so romantic, and the price so incredibly low, that this is a marvelous choice for the the tourist with a Bohemian spirit who likes to travel on a budget.

VILLA '600
Proprietor: Stefano
30012 Isola Torcello
Venice, Italy
tel: (041) 730 999
4 simple rooms - inexpensive
Exceptional budget value
On a small island near Venice

The Hotel due Torri is not a cozy little inn, but it is very unique in its own way. You enter into an enormous central inner court which is almost like a football field - a football field with a floor of large rust and cream colored tile that looks like a chessboard.   Encircling the room are columns supporting arches which form an arcade.   The ceiling is covered with brilliant paintings. Bright green and red comfortable lounge chairs form small groupings for conversation. After the initial impact, the room begins to "grow on you." Especially when you read the history and realize that in the 14th century the Lords of Verona used this building as their official guest house.

The bedrooms are even more unusual than the lobby.   Each has genuine antique furniture meticulously collected to maintain authenticity.   Each of the bedrooms has a different decor.   Most feature very ornate furnishings.   Some of the rooms are Louis XVI style, others Greek-Roman, others Charles X period, others English.   But all are real antiques!   To make this choice of rooms even more fun, there is a set of slides in the lobby where you can look at the pictures of the various rooms and pick out one that especially suits your mood.   (If the hotel is not filled, of course!)

HOTEL DUE TORRI
Owner: Enrico Wallner
Piazza San Anastasia
37100 Verona, Italy
tel:(45) 595 044   telex:480524
100 rooms - expensive
Authentic antiques used throughout
Located in the heart of Verona

The entrance to the Hotel Victoria is starkly modern - almost with a museum-like quality.   The white walls, white ceiling, white floors, and an enormous skylight are softened by the green plants.   At first glance I was disappointed since I had heard so many glowing reports of the merits of this small hotel. However, the mood begins to change as you enter the reception area with its Oriental carpets, and, by the time you arrive into the lounge area the feeling is definitely moving toward the antique ambiance with the original heavy ancient wooden beams and one of the original stone walls exposed, leather chairs, and some lovely antique tables. The bedrooms are extremely modern and beautifully functional with good reading lights, comfortable chairs, and excellent bathrooms.

The Victoria actually dates back to ancient times and the new hotel is built within the shell of an ancient building.   The architect even incorporated some of the archaeologically interesting finds of the site into a museum in the basement level.   When the hotel is not full and all of the dining room tables are not needed, special "windows" open up on the floor of the restaurant and the museum below is lit so that you can study the artifacts as you dine!

HOTEL VICTORIA
Rodolfo Zema, Manager
Via Adua, 8
37121 Verona, Italy
tel: (45) 594 939   telex: 431109
44 rooms - moderate
Breakfast only, Credit card: AX

The Hotel Turm belongs to the Romantik Hotel Chain.   Just being a member of this exclusive "club" indicates the hotel is pretty special because to belong the inn must have the owner personally involved in the management and the interior must have an antique ambiance.   The Hotel Turm is no exception.   There is an especially attractive little dining room with vaulted white washed ceilings and chalet-style rustic wooden furniture.   There are a few antiques in the hallways and lounges.   The bedrooms are simple, but very pleasant with light pine furniture and fluffy down comforters on the beds.   There is a swimming pool on the terrace where one can swim or lounge by the pool while gazing out to the little town and the mountains beyond.   There is even a small indoor pool.

The Hotel Turm dates back to the 13th century and Mr. Pramstrahler takes great care to maintain touches of the "olde worlde" charm by interspersing antique chests, cradles, chairs, and ancient artifacts.

HOTEL TURM
Owner: Family Pramstrahler
1-39050 Vols am Schlern
Sudtirol, Italy
tel: (0471) 72 014
24 rooms - moderate
Closed Nov. to end of Dec.
Credit cards: AX, Vs

Indoor and outdoor pools
Mountain setting NE Bolzano

HOTEL NAME & ADDRESS - clearly printed or typed

Vi prego di voler riservare: *I would like to request:*

_____   Numero delle camere con bagno o doccia privata
                    Number of rooms with private bath/shower

_____   Numero delle camere senza bagno o doccia
                    Number of rooms without private bath/shower

_____   Numero delle persone nel nostro gruppo
                    Number of persons in our party

_____   Data di arrivo   _____   Data di partenza
                    Arrival date   *Departure date*

Vi prego inoltre de fornirmi le seguenti informazioni:
Please let me know as soon as possible the following:

Potete riservare le camere richieste?   SI   NO
Can your reserve the space requested?   *yes*   *no*

Prezzo giornaliero
Rate per night   _____

I pasti sono compresi nel prezzo?   SI   NO
Are meals included in your rate?   *yes*   *no*

E necessario un deposito?   SI   NO
Do you need a deposit?   *yes*   *no*

Quanto e necessario come deposito?
How much deposit do you need?   _____

Ringraziando anticipatamente, porgo distinti saluti,
Thanking you in advance, I send my best regards,

YOUR NAME & ADDRESS - clearly printed or typed

Index

Alphabetical Listing of Hotels by Hotel Name

HOTEL	TOWN	MAP #	Page#
FLORENCE, Hotel	Bellagio	19	106
FORUM, Hotel	Rome	41	31 157
GAIDELLO CLUB	Castelfranco	29	113
GASTHOF OBEREGGEN	Obereggen	7	140
GUILIA, Pensione	Gargnano	14	130
GRAND HOTEL DEI CASTELLI	Sestri Levante	28	165
GRAND EXCELSIOR VITTORIA	Sorrento	45	32 176
GRAND HOTEL QUISIANA	Capri	44	34 111
GRAND HOTEL VILLA IGIEA	Sicily, Palermo	52	94 167
GRAND HOTEL VILLA SERBELLONI	Bellagio	19	50 107
GRAND HOTEL VILLA CORA	Florence	30	121
GREGORIANA, Hotel	Rome	41	158
GRIFONE, Hotel	Sirmione	15	174
GRITTI PALACE, Hotel	Venice	1	27 181
HASSLER, Hotel	Rome	41	159
HERMITAGE, Hotel	Florence	30	122
IL CAPRICORNO	Sauze D'Oulx	24	164
IL PELLICANO	Porto Ercole	40	146
IL SAN PIETRO DI POSITANO	Positano	46	150
LA BADIA	Orvieto	39	62 141
LA CISTERNA	San Gimignano	34	66 162
LA FENICE ET DES ARTISTES	Venice	1	182
LE SIRENUSE HOTEL	Positano	46	149
LE TRE VASELLE	Torgiano	38	61 178
LOCANDA CIPRIANI TORCELLO	Venice-Torcello	1	186
LOCANDA DELL'AMOROSA	Sinalunga	36	64 173
LUNA, Hotel	Capri	44	112

HOTEL	TOWN	MAP #	Page #
LUNGARNO HOTEL	Florence	30	29 123
MARINO ALLA SCALA	Milan	21	75 137
MARMORATA HOTEL	Ravello	47	152
MENARDI, Hotel	Cortina	5	42 118
MONNA LISA, Pensione	Florence	30	124
NAZIONALE, Hotel	Portofino	27	147
PALAZZO RAVIZZA, Pensione	Siena	35	172
PALUMBO, Hotel	Ravello	47	82 153
PITRIZZA	Sardinia, Porto Cervo	53	163
PUNTA EST, Hotel	Finale Ligure	25	120
REGENCY, Hotel	Florence	30	125
RELAIS EL TOULA	Ponzano	3	145
ROMANTIK HOTEL TURM	Vols	9	190
SAN DOMENICO PALACE	Sicily, Taormina	51	168
SANTAVENERE, Hotel	Maratea	49	133
SEGUSO, Pensione	Venice	1	183
SOLE, Hotel	Riva del Garda	13	156
SPLENDIDO, Hotel	Portofino	27	72 148
STEFANER, Pension	Tiers	8	177
SUBASIO, Hotel	Assisi	37	59 103
TENUTA DI RICAVO	Castellini in Chianti	33	114
TIMEO, Hotel	Sicily, Taormina	51	91 169
UMBRA, Hotel	Assisi	37	104
VALADIER, Hotel	Rome	41	161
VERBANO, Hotel	Isola dei Pescatori	22	52 144
VICTORIA, Hotel	Verona	16	189
VIGILJOCH, Hotel	Merano-Lana	11	136

HOTEL	TOWN	MAP #	Page #
VILLA '600	Venice-Torcello	1	187
VILLA CASALECCHI	Castellina in Chianti	33	115
VILLA CIMBRONE	Ravello	47	154
VILLA CIPRIANI	Asolo	4	39 101
VILLA CONSULMER	Mogliano	2	138
VILLA CORTINE PALACE, Hotel	Sirmione	15	24 175
VILLA D'ESTE	Cernobbio	20	116
VILLA FIORIO	Grottaferrata	42	131
VILLA LA MASSA, Hotel	Florence-Candeli	30	126
VILLA LA PRINCIPESSA, Hotel	Lucca	31	71 132
VILLA LE BARONE	Panzano	32	65 142
VILLA MARIA, Pensione	Ravello	47	155
VILLA SAN MICHELE	Florence-Fiesole	30	128
VILLA SANT'ANDREA	Sicily, Taormina	51	170
VILLA VILLORESI	Florence-Colonnata	30	127

Index

Alphabetical Listing of Hotels by Town Name

TOWN	HOTEL	MAP #		Page #
FLORENCE	Hermitage, Pensione	30		122
FLORENCE	Lungarno Hotel	30	29	123
FLORENCE	Monna Lisa, Pensione	30		124
FLORENCE	Regency, Hotel	30		125
FLORENCE-CANDELI	Villa La Massa, Hotel	30		126
FLORENCE-COLONNATA	Villa Villoresi	30		127
✗FLORENCE-FIESOLE	Villa San Michele	30		128
GARGNANO	Baia D'Oro, Pensione	14	47	129
GARGNANO	Giulia, Pensione	14		130
GROTTAFERRATA	Villa Fiorio	42		131
LUCCA	Villa la Principessa, Hotel	31	71	132
MARATEA	Santavenere, Hotel	49		133
✗MERANO	Castel Frieberg, Hotel	11	46	134
✗MERANO	Castel Labers, Hotel	11		135
MERANO	Vigiljoch, Hotel	11		136
MILAN	Marino alla Scala	21		137
✗MOGLIANO	Villa Condulmer	2		138
OBEREGGEN	Bewallerhof, Hotel	7	44	139
OBEREGGEN	Gastof Obereggen	7		140
ORVIETO	La Badia	39	62	141
PANZANO	Villa le Barone	32		142
✗PERGINE	Castel Pergine	12		143
PESCATORI (Isola dei)	Verbano, Hotel	22	52	144
PONZANO	Relais El Toula	3		145
PORTO ERCOLE	Il Pellicano	40		146
PORTOFINO	Nazionale, Hotel	27		147
PORTOFINO	Splendido, Hotel	27	72	148

TOWN	HOTEL	MAP #	Page #
POSITANO	Le Sirenuse Hotel	46	149
POSITANO	Il San Pietro di Positano	46	150
RAVELLO	Caruso Belvedere, Hotel	47	151
RAVELLO	Marmorato Hotel	47	152
RAVELLO	Palumbo, Hotel	47 82	153
RAVELLO	Villa Cimbrone	47	154
RAVELLO	Villa Maria, Pensione	48	155
RIVA DEL GARDA	Sole, Hotel	13	156
ROME	Forum, Hotel	41 31	157
ROME	Gregoriana, Hotel	41	158
ROME	Hassler, Hotel	41	159
ROME	D'Inghilterra, Hotel	41	160
ROME	Valadier Hotel	41	161
SAN GIMIGNANO	La Cisterna	34 66	162
SARDINIA, PORTO CERVO	Pitrizza	53	163
SAUZE D'OULX	Il Capricorno	24	164
SESTRI LEVANTE	Grand Hotel dei Castelli	28	165
SEXTEN	Berghotel Tirol	6	166
SICILY, PALERMO	Grand Hotel Villa Igiea	52	167
SICILY, TAORMINA	San Domenico Palace	51	168
SICILY, TAORMINA	Timeo, Hotel	51 91	169
SICILY, TAORMINA	Villa Sant'Andrea	51	170
SIENA	Certosa Di Maggiano	35	171
SIENA	Palazzo Ravizza, Pensione	35	172
SINALUNGA	Locanda dell'Amorosa	36 64	173
SIRMIONE	Grifone, Hotel	15	174
SIRMIONE	Villa Cortine Palace, Hotel	15 24	175

TOWN	HOTEL	MAP #	Page #
SORRENTO	Grand Excelsior Vittoria	45	32 176
TIERS	Stefaner, Pensione	8	177
TORGIANO	Le Tre Vaselle	38	61 178
TROPEA-PARAGHELIA	Baia Paraelios	50	89 179
VENICE	Do Pozzi, Hotel	1	180
VENICE	Gritti Palace, Hotel	1	27 181
VENICE	La Fenice et Des Artistes	1	182
VENICE	Seguso, Pensione	1	183
VENICE-GIUDECCI	Cipriani, Hotel	1	184
VENICE-LIDO	Quattro Fontane	1	185
VENICE-TORCELLO	Locanda Cipriani Torcello	1	186
VENICE-TORCELLO	Villa '600	1	187
VERONA	Due Torri, Hotel	1	26 188
VERONA	Victoria, Hotel	16	189
VOLS	Romantik Hotel Turm	9	190

"INN DISCOVERIES FROM OUR READERS"

Future editions of KAREN BROWN'S COUNTRY INN SERIES are going to include a new feature - a list of hotels recommended by our readers. We have received many letters describing wonderful inns you have discovered; however, we have never included them until we had the opportunity to make a personal inspection. This seemed a waste of some marvelous "tips". So we have started a file to be used in each forthcoming edition of our guide books which will be called "INN DISCOVERIES FROM OUR READERS".

If you have a favorite discovery you would be willing to share with other travellers who love to travel the "inn way" please let us hear from you and include the following information.

l. Your name, address and telephone number

2. Name, address, and telephone of "Your Inn"

3. Brochure or picture of inn (we cannot return photographs)

4. Written permission to use an edited version of your description

5. Would you want your name and city included in the book?

In addition to our current guide books which include hotels in France, England, Scotland, Wales, Switzerland, and Italy, we are now researching guide books for all of Europe and would appreciate comments on any of your favorites. The type of inn we would love to hear about are those with special "Olde Worlde" ambiance, charm, and atmosphere. We need a brochure or picture so that we can select those which most closely follow the mood of our guides. We look forward to hearing from you. Thank you very much!

KAREN BROWN has spent most of her life in the San Francisco Bay area where she now lives with her devoted German Shepherd, "Andy", in a cozy cottage surrounded by her collection of antiques. When nineteen Karen traveled to Europe where she wrote *French Country Inns and Chateau Hotels* - the first book in what has grown to be an extremely successful series on charming small European hotels. When not writing, Karen has worked as a travel consultant and as a tour guide to Europe. She loves skiing, hiking, cooking, and entertaining. Another hobby is languages. Karen speaks fluent French and German. Her real love though is exploring the world and although she has traveled extensively, staying in a wide variety of accommodations ranging from tents in the Himalayas to safari camps in Africa, her favorite abode is still the small country inn of Europe which she captures so delightfully in her books.

Notes

Notes

Notes

Notes

Notes

Notes

Notes

Notes

Notes

Notes

Notes

Notes